Ethics in the Post-Enron Age

Iris Stuart

California State University at Fullerton

Bruce Stuart

California State University at Fullerton

THOMSON

SOUTH-WESTERN

Australia · Canada · Mexico · Singapore · Spain · United Kingdom · United States

THOMSON

SOUTH-WESTERN

Ethics in the Post-Enron Age

Iris Stuart and Bruce Stuart

VP/Editorial Director:
Jack W. Calhoun

VP/Editor-in-Chief:
George Werthman

Acquisitions Editor:
Julie Lindsay

Developmental Editor:
Janice Hughes

Marketing Manager:
Keith Chassé

Production Editor:
Heather Mann

Manufacturing Coordinator:
Doug Wilke

Design Project Manager:
Tippy McIntosh

Cover Designer:
Tippy McIntosh

Cover Images:
© PhotoDisc, Inc.

Printer:
Globus Printing
Minster, OH

For permission to use material from this
text or product, contact us by
Tel (800) 730-2214
Fax (800) 730-2215
http://www.thomsonrights.com

For more information
contact South-Western,
5191 Natorp Boulevard,
Mason, Ohio, 45040.
Or you can visit our Internet site at:
http://www.swlearning.com

Preface

REFORM IN ACCOUNTING EDUCATION: THE ROLE OF WRITING AND DISCUSSION IN ETHICS

Recent accounting scandals involving high-profile companies such as Enron, WorldCom, and Arthur Andersen have called into question accounting practices and undermined public confidence in the profession. These events challenge leaders in accounting education to implement reform and make conscientious efforts to improve ethics education in the professional development of accountants.

In the 1990s, the Accounting Education Change Commission (AECC) sought to "inspire depth of learning and the students' appreciation of accounting education as a life-long process..." and to enhance students' "competence for dealing with complex and unstructured 'real world' situations." In response to ethical scandals in government and business, the AECC supported a curriculum that helps students learn the concepts and principles underlying accounting rules. Because the recent business crisis involves accountants engaged in questionable business practices, this casebook helps students to recognize ethical dilemmas and moral problems that present themselves in the "messy" world of accounting. As students develop technical knowledge and basic skills of accounting practice, they also "should know and understand the ethics of the profession and be able to make value-based judgments."[1]

In order to meet this goal, we advocate that students in the earliest stages of accounting education learn to analyze business information, think clearly about its presentation, and demonstrate their decision-making abilities through written and oral argument. Students will learn financial reporting principles and become more aware of how business information is used when they are expected to write and discuss the steps by which they have applied accounting concepts and made accounting judgments in specific case studies. A model for ethical decision making is outlined in Chapter 1 to give students a process by which they can make the most informed accounting decisions. Steps include identifying an ethical dilemma and its features, analyzing available and responsible solutions, and resolving the dilemma by selecting the best alternative. In this way, students experience a "real life" dimension in learning where actions and their consequences are considered. *Ethics in the Post-Enron Age* allows students to form solid analytical communication skills by writing and discussing the logic used to reach a solution to the dilemma in an effort to clarify their own thoughts and develop the intellectual habits of professional competence.

Instructors are aware of students' difficulties in coping with the ethical problems that arise in complex transactions. Facing uncertainty in applying accounting principles to clarify economic transactions and provide relevant information for decision making, the accountant experiences pressures that challenge his or her judgment and make it difficult to act with integrity and for the public good. For example, disagreements between accountant and client over the preparation of financial statements often pose moral questions. The accountant may be tempted to compromise professional responsibilities in order to meet company standards of financial performance. The classroom setting offers the opportunity for the instructor to help students to become aware of ethical dilemmas and to gain confidence in addressing their complexity as a normal part of their professional duties.

The casebook includes more than 150 ethical dilemmas appropriate for use in Financial Accounting, Intermediate Accounting, Auditing, Fraud Detection, and Internal Auditing courses at both the undergraduate and graduate level. The cases are organized into six chapters with two or three subsections per chapter. Chapter 1, Accounting Ethics in the Contemporary Business Climate, includes a decision-making model to use in evaluating the ethical dilemmas. Chapter 2, The Income Statement, includes cases on revenue recognition, expense recognition, and earnings misstatements. Chapter 3, The Balance Sheet, includes cases related to assets and liabilities and owners' equity. Chapter 4, Corporate Governance, includes ethical dilemmas related to company expenditures, independence issues and corporate decisions, and company pension plans. Chapter 5, Financial Statement Reporting and Disclosure, includes ethical dilemmas related to financial statement disclosure, pro forma reporting, and footnote and supplemental disclosures. Chapter 6, Management Fraud and Accounting Choice, includes cases on earnings restatements, management fraud, and accounting choices. Chapter 7, Professional Conduct in Accounting, includes cases on audit failures, the AICPA Code of Professional Conduct, and tax and audit clients. The cases vary in length from one paragraph to several pages. The shorter cases are useful for brief class discussions. The longer cases are appropriate for team projects, longer assignments, and more extended classroom discussions.

Each chapter includes cases based on real-world companies (e.g., Enron, WorldCom, Tyco, Adelphia, Qwest, Sunbeam) and cases based on hypothetical companies developed from the author's work experience. Each case poses an ethical dilemma associated with an accounting decision, so the student's knowledge of accounting principles and ability to recognize and resolve ethical dilemmas are enriched and developed.

Specific use for cases, with suggested course syllabi, is noted in the Instructor's Manual that is posted on the book's site at http://stuart.swlearning.com.

Endnotes

---

[1] The Accounting Education Change Commission, *Position Statement Number One,* "Objectives of Education for Accountants," September 1990.

Chapter 1
Accounting Ethics in the Contemporary Business Climate

TODAY'S HEADLINES

"Enron reports $638 million in losses and a $1.2 billion reduction in shareholder equity." "The SEC opens an inquiry into Enron's related party transactions." "New documents show Enron traders manipulated California energy costs." "The Enron debacle spotlights huge void in financial regulation." "Arthur Andersen, a Big Five audit firm, is subpoenaed by the SEC, related to the Enron audit." "Justice Department steps up Andersen investigation." "Andersen verdict: 'Guilty'." "Andersen is toast."

During the 1990s, Enron, a Houston-based marketer of electricity, gas, and oil, recorded spectacular growth and skyrocketing stock prices, but in 2001, SEC investigations, declining stock prices, executive indictments, and bankruptcy rocked the company. Thousands of employees were fired and those heavily invested in company stock lost most of their retirement savings. Enron's auditor, Arthur Andersen, a Big Five accounting firm, also came under SEC investigation and was convicted of obstruction of justice when evidence proved the firm shredded damaging Enron documents.

With Andersen's advice and support, Enron moved expenses to off-balance sheet accounts, thus masking its debt from lending institutions and potential investors. These "second party corporate entities" hid Enron's losses. Andersen's role and subsequent conviction forced the sale of its many international offices, the loss of major clients, and finally the loss of its license to audit.

These highly publicized scandals suggested a market economy out of control and raised demands for more effective government regulation. The public asked: "What shall we do when even the auditors fail to perform their jobs with competence and integrity?"

THE BUSINESS CRISIS AND ACCOUNTING EDUCATION

The contemporary challenge for you as accounting students is to prepare for a global economy of multinational corporations and international stock markets. Soon you will function in a marketplace of rapid change that will test your knowledge and skills. Your professional tasks will be complicated by innovative business practices, the large-scale scope of corporate activity, and the economic impact of corporate decision-making that will place powerful pressures on your judgment. In this complex business scene, various interested parties—owners, workers, and investors—will challenge your competence and confront your integrity.

Corporate corruption and executive dishonesty can pollute the business atmosphere in which you will perform your professional duties. You may confront narrow self-interest, greed, and deception in the form of cooked books, insider trading, pro forma earnings, and risk management that calculates the cost of fraud. You may face contemporary companies that use aggressive accounting practices to misrepresent their earnings and may deal with executives who misuse their companies' funds. You may encounter corporate boards that neglect their oversight functions and even auditors who fail to disclose wrongdoing.

In view of such business scandals, there is a public outcry for businesses and accounting firms to be ethically responsible in their transactions and in the use of business information. Commentators demand managerial honesty in sharing information with boards, shareholders, and government agencies. Shareholders and boards want managers to work for the best interests of the company not for their own individualized interests. The public demands corporate transparency in press releases and informal earnings projections; full disclosure in official earnings reports is an even higher priority.[1] As accountants, you must face these challenges with technical competence and integrity.

As lists of company executives "in hot water" are released, you might ask about their education. Did they receive any ethics training as they learned the techniques of their occupations and the strategies for business success? If so, did their moral education simply not match the sophistication and complexity of their technical training or the rapid pace of change in the contemporary business world? Were these people not educated to follow the rules of their craft, to perform according to the principles of their profession? And what of the accountants who are caught up in these corporate scandals? What is their responsibility? Have they been acting unethically? What lessons in (and out of) school should they have been learning all along?

In such an atmosphere, accounting education must go beyond mere technical training and "learning the rules" to include a foundation for grasping the basic concepts and principles of the profession. You must understand the ethics of the profession and become responsible for making value-based judgments in the performance of your duties.

ETHICAL REFORM IN ACCOUNTING EDUCATION

As you learn to identify with the accounting profession and develop the technical knowledge and basic skills of accounting practice, you will also learn the values of the profession. The Accounting Education Change Commission (AECC) advises faculty about goals for accounting undergraduates: "They should know and understand the ethics of the profession and be able to make value-based judgments."[2] In order to meet this goal, we advocate an approach that emphasizes the importance of your learning at the earliest stages of accounting education to analyze business information, to think clearly about its presentation, and to demonstrate responsibility for business decision-making through written and oral argument.

A case study approach gives high priority to the development of analytical skills and good communication. This casebook encourages you to give reasons and explanations for potential resolutions; in doing this, you will gain a foundation for making ethical judgments in your professional conduct. As you work with the cases in this text, be reminded that there are several codes of conduct created by professional societies that outline accountants' proper working relationships to firm, client, and the broad public interest. Several of these codes govern accounting practice in the United States, including those published by the American Institute of Certified Public Accountants (AICPA), the Institute of Management Accountants (IMA), the Institute of Internal Auditors (IIA), and the Securities and Exchange Commission (SEC.) These professional codes emphasize ethical decisions accountants make in the performance of their duties, and these codes should be the foundation for your own ethical judgments. Whatever the nature of the ethical questions that you face and the pressures that confront your judgment, the codes and generally accepted accounting principles ask you to act with integrity for the public good.

The cases that follow will include information that is crucial for identifying the business information needing clarification and the accounting issues to be resolved. Determine which information is significant and which accounting issues are at stake. Note the various parties in the situation and where their interests may lie. It is likely that one party or another benefits (or is harmed) by the accountant's decision, yet the accountant's professional obligation is to make principled, rational decisions. As an accountant, it is important to be prepared to give a written and/or an oral report of your findings, decisions, and reasoning. Specifically, these cases will give you practice in written and oral argumentation.

FINANCIAL REPORTING: RELEVANCE AND RELIABILITY

To respond to the AECC's call for reform in undergraduate accounting education, accounting curriculum should explore the dilemmas posed by certain financial transactions and business reporting decisions. An ethical decision-making model will help you identify the moral aspects of financial transactions and the ethical problems that emerge as you work to fairly represent a firm's financial position.

As we have mentioned, the basic patterns of financial reporting are established by professional standards that encompass accounting concepts and principles, technical procedures, and codes of professional conduct. Comprehensive expression of these standards is found in the Financial Accounting Standards Board (FASB) publications. In our ethical decision-making model, we focus on several main characteristics of financial reporting, which illustrate the primary responsibility of accounting in the modern corporate system as summarized by the Financial Accounting Standards Board (FASB):

> "Financial reporting should provide information that is useful to present
> and potential investors and creditors and other users in making rational

investment, credit, and similar decisions. The information should be comprehensible to those who have a reasonable understanding of business and economic activities and are willing to study the information with reasonable diligence."[3]

Given this fundamental responsibility of the accountant, FASB has described criteria by which accounting choices must be judged. These qualitative characteristics of accounting information are the ingredients that make information useful and represent the objectives that should be achieved when accounting decisions are made. When you, as an accountant, examine business transactions and face particular uncertainties—even ethical dilemmas—these qualitative ingredients play a crucial role in the decision process that will lead to appropriate accounting judgments.

When addressing the business situation, the accountant asks: *What characteristics improve the quality of information that is disclosed?* The answer shapes all accounting decisions that follow: *The information must be both **relevant** and **reliable***.

Relevant information is information that reduces the uncertainties of a situation. It reflects the financial reality of the situation and improves the user's capacity to make a decision based on the information. Often, relevant information provides a clear view of a previous financial situation that is useful for predicting the future. Relevant accounting decisions are also timely; that is, they make information available while it has the capacity to influence decisions.

An accounting decision should also be **reliable**; that is, it should faithfully represent what it claims to represent. In accounting, events represented are economic resources, transactions, and obligations. Reliability also includes **verifiability**, measured as a consensus among independent parties using the same methods. Reliability also includes **neutrality**, that is, the presentation of information that is free from bias toward a particular result. Neutral information can be used by anyone and is not biased toward one particular audience. Basically, accounting information that is reliable will report economic activity that faithfully represents the situation, without coloring the image for the purpose of influencing behavior toward one particular direction.[4]

A MODEL FOR ETHICAL DECISION-MAKING

The first step in resolving an unclear situation is to recognize the ethical dilemma you are facing. When generally accepted accounting procedures (GAAP) do not tell you how to resolve the accounting issue (either because there are several conflicting rules or because there are no GAAP rules), you face a moral dilemma. In such circumstances, be alert to pressures on the reporting process that may be due to the self-interested behavior of the interested parties (an interested party is an individual or a group that is affected by the financial transaction or its disclosure in the financial statement). In all cases, prepare a financial statement that fairly reports the financial position of the firm by resolving the moral dilemma through an orderly process of inquiry and rational analysis.

Some ethical issues may be resolved by one right answer. In other circumstances, examination of the issues may suggest more than one appropriate answer. When this happens, evaluate each option and select the best or the most ethical alternative. Note that the process of determining the most ethical alternative includes posing questions intended to identify all the significant facts of the business situation. These include the interests of the immediate parties, the GAAP principles that are relevant for resolving the situation, and a realistic appraisal of the possible consequences of the decision.

The ethics model is described in Table 1. The following steps will help you make decisions involving ethical dilemmas.

Ethics Model

Identification

1. Know when you have a problem. You may face an ethical dilemma when you are aware of the potential harm or benefit of your accounting decisions on the parties involved. A dilemma occurs when this awareness is combined with the inability to clearly apply accounting principles in order to represent truthfully the economic reality of the situation.

Analysis

2. Move toward an ethical resolution by identifying and analyzing the principal elements in the situation. Seek answers to the following questions in this sequence:
   a. What parties (interested individuals or groups) may be harmed or benefited?
   b. Whose rights or claims may be violated?
   c. What specific interests are in conflict?
   d. What are my responsibilities and obligations?

3. Identify the alternatives and weigh the impact of each alternative on the interested parties. What alternative methods are available to report the transaction, situation, or event? What is the effect of each alternative on the various parties? Which individuals or groups are harmed or benefited most? Evaluate the **relevance** and **reliability** of the alternatives. Potential bias must be identified; questions of timeliness should be considered. Does the report fairly represent the economic reality it claims to describe? Would another accountant or interested party measure the information and reach the same result? Has the accountant successfully resisted pressures to predetermine the results of his or her accounting judgments?

Table 1

Ethics Model

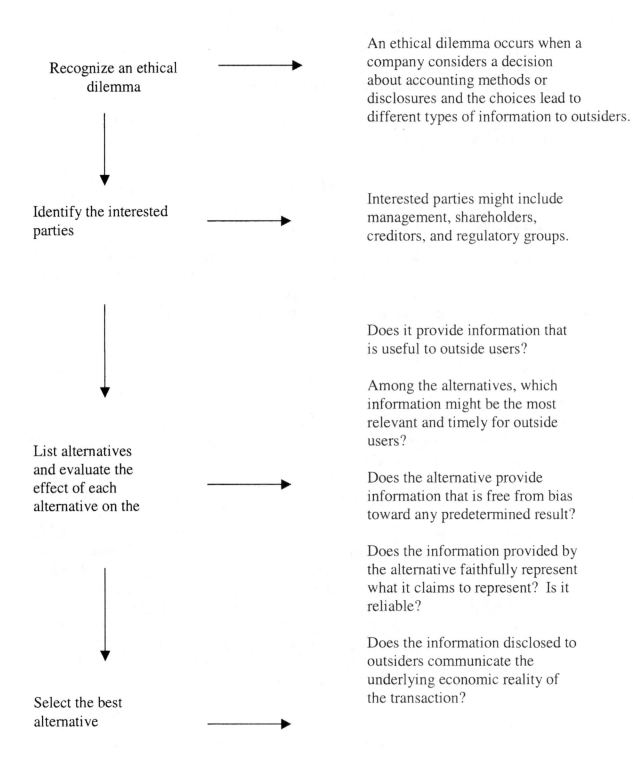

Recognize an ethical dilemma ⟶ An ethical dilemma occurs when a company considers a decision about accounting methods or disclosures and the choices lead to different types of information to outsiders.

Identify the interested parties ⟶ Interested parties might include management, shareholders, creditors, and regulatory groups.

Does it provide information that is useful to outside users?

Among the alternatives, which information might be the most relevant and timely for outside users?

List alternatives and evaluate the effect of each alternative on the ⟶ Does the alternative provide information that is free from bias toward any predetermined result?

Does the information provided by the alternative faithfully represent what it claims to represent? Is it reliable?

Does the information disclosed to outsiders communicate the underlying economic reality of the transaction?

Select the best alternative ⟶

Resolution

4. Select the best or most ethical alternative, considering all the circumstances and the consequences.

The accountant must consider the moral and social implications of decisions beyond maximizing shareholder wealth. He or she must determine how the decisions affect all parties with interests in the company. Interested parties include shareholders, debtholders, employees, suppliers, customers, the local community, and any other party that may be affected by the accounting decision or that may use the information to make economic decisions. Why should you be concerned about each of these interested parties? Because it will help you develop a complete analysis of the decision and expand your perspective beyond immediately affected parties. In other words, awareness of interested parties and how they might be harmed or might benefit in business transactions and accounting judgments will enable you to perform the appropriate accounting task within the complex corporate system of today's business world.

CONCLUSION

The ethics cases that follow will ask why you consider particular facts in each case to be important and why particular GAAP principles are relevant for reporting the transaction. The practice of giving reasons and explaining how you reached your conclusions should help you develop the discipline of proceeding step-by-step in a clear, rational process of decision-making.

Chapters 2 and 3 focus on ethics cases related to the income statement and the balance sheet. The financial statements should accurately represent the economic situation of the company, but various interested parties have incentives to mislead the public, including investors. These cases offer you the opportunity to apply generally accepted accounting principles as you recognize the various interests of the parties involved.

Chapter 4 discusses corporate governance concerns and the manner in which companies are regulated through government regulation, industry regulation, or self-regulation. The failure of effective governance to protect interested parties against manipulation of disclosed information is a serious problem in today's business environment. Such deception by management hampers the ability of the users of financial statements from gaining accurate business information for decision-making and leaves their interests unprotected.

Chapter 5 concentrates on information in the annual report. Are the reporting methods and disclosures accurate, sufficient, and reasonably presented? Do the statements and disclosures meet the generally accepted accounting principles? Cases cover both annual and quarterly reports, as well as pro forma earnings releases, and challenge you to determine whether management has complied with the basic concepts and principles of accounting practice and released information that expresses the economic situation of the company.

Chapter 6 acknowledges the significant problems of management fraud and the complexities of accounting choice when significant pressures are brought to bear on the disclosure process. The cases involve falsifying company performance to secure loans or honor debt covenants, to meet Wall Street analysts' income projections, and to achieve earnings targets (and thereby assure management bonuses or stock options).

Chapter 7 addresses the principles and guidelines that are expressed in the codes of professional conduct. Are you able to recognize your professional responsibilities in particular circumstances? Can you resist the pressures to ignore the technical and ethical demands of the profession?

By working through the ethics cases in each chapter, employing the accounting principles, and making use of the ethics model, you should have a worthy challenge in identifying and resolving ethical dilemmas.

Endnotes

[1] David Vogel, "Recycling Corporate Responsibility," *The Wall Street Journal,* August 20, 2002; Rushworth M. Kidder, "Orange County Commentary: How to Succeed in Business? Try Ethics," *The Los Angeles Times,* July 14, 2002.

[2] The Accounting Education Change Commission, *Position Statement Number One,* "Objectives of Education for Accountants," September 1990.

[3] *Original Pronouncements: Accounting Standards* (New York: John Wiley and Sons, Inc. 2001–2002 edition), III, Concept One, paragraph 34, p. 1014.

[4] *Original Pronouncements: Accounting Standards* (New York: John Wiley and Sons, Inc. 2001–2002 edition), III, p. 1022; FASB, paragraphs 46, 47, 48, 56, 63, 77, 81; pp. 48–49, 51–53, 56–59.

Chapter 2
The Income Statement

It is crucial to identify the accounting and ethical issues related to the income statement. This is because company performance is often measured by revenue growth and net income. Management interests may be advanced by overstating revenue or understating expense. For example, management compensation may be connected to company performance, and management may encourage accounting practices that falsify net income. Whenever this happens, outside parties (including investors) may be misled to overestimate company performance. In some instances, Wall Street analysts may project a company's net income, and management may "adjust" the income statement to analysts' predictions, thereby attempting to avoid stock price decline. Such manipulations to increase revenue or reduce expense will not reflect the true economic situation of the company.

Problems related to the income statement are presented in three categories: (1) revenue recognition, (2) expense recognition, and (3) earnings misstatements.

REVENUE RECOGNITION

Case 2.1
Qwest Communications International, Inc.

In July 2002, Qwest, a telecommunications company based in Denver, Colorado, acknowledged that it improperly recorded revenue for 2000, 2001, and 2002. Qwest provides local telecommunication services, wireless services, and directory services for a 14-state service area in the upper Midwest and the northwestern part of the United States. The company restated its financial results for 2000 and 2001 and reduced its estimate of earnings for 2002.[1] The company's earnings before restatement were reported as a net loss of $81 million for 2000 and a $3.96 billion net loss for 2001.[2]

With 61,000 employees and yearly sales revenue of $19.7 billion in 2001, Qwest provides telecommunication services to residential, business, and government customers. The company reports financial information in the following business segments: retail services, wholesale services, network services, and directory services. Its revenue misstatements originated from the company's handling of revenue from transactions where it sold long-term capacity on its network and bought similar capacity from its trading partners (referred to as swap transactions or round-trip trades).

Arthur Andersen, LLP, advised several telecommunications clients on how to structure swap transactions in a 48-page document referred to as the "white paper." [3] According to the document, swap transactions are not barter arrangements, which would prevent the two firms from recognizing revenue. The document suggests that two given companies structure their transactions so the capacity sold is an operating asset and the capacity bought is a capital asset. This allows the seller to recognize revenue and to record the cost of providing the capacity as a capitalized cost rather than an expense, moving the cost off the income statement and putting it in a capital asset account on the balance sheet. From Andersen's point of view, because the risks and rewards of buying capital leases were different than those of operating leases, the companies involved in the swaps were no longer exchanging similar assets. If the assets exchanged were not similar, it was possible to recognize revenue on the capacity swapped in the transaction.

Companies in the telecommunications industry relied heavily on the use of swap accounting to inflate revenue, which was commonly believed to be the most reliable measure of a company's health. These companies included Qwest, Global Crossing, and WorldCom. Arthur Andersen was the auditor for many telecommunications firms. SEC officials were concerned that such revenue-increasing tactics were widely used by telecommunications companies to "give the appearance of economic activity and growth when there was none."[4] These companies, in effect, were following advice similar to that given in the Andersen "white paper." The SEC officials believed that such round-trip transactions by telecommunications companies had no business purpose other than to increase revenue.

In August 2002, the SEC formally concluded that the telecommunications companies improperly booked revenue from capacity swaps with other companies. This SEC decision officially puts an end to the widely used industry practice that had inflated revenue for many telecommunications companies.[5] The ruling resulted in earnings restatements by several companies and prompted shareholder lawsuits alleging accounting fraud. (From an accounting perspective, errors are "unintentional misstatements," whereas fraud is characterized as "intentional misstatements," arising from fraudulent financial reporting or misappropriation of assets.)

Telecommunications firms are expected to argue that their accounting treatment for swap transactions was made in good faith based on the guidance given by their auditors. Under these conditions, the restatement does not indicate fraudulent activity on the part of executives, since there was no guidance in the accounting regulations for the recording of the swap transactions. However, due to the attention given the situation, Qwest stock dropped 85 percent in 2002, from a high of about $52.00 in September 2000 to $3.16 in September 2002.

Joseph Nacchio, the chief executive officer of Qwest, resigned under pressure in June 2002. Nacchio and other top executives at Qwest had sold Qwest stock during the years the swap accounting was used. Nacchio's stock sales alone netted $130 million in profit. Qwest insiders sold stock worth $530 million between January 2000 and July 2001, raising questions about their interest in keeping the stock price as high as possible by reporting growth in sales revenue.[6]

Due to the change in revenue recognition methods, Qwest is in danger of violating a debt covenant for $4 billion in loans from J.P. Morgan Chase and Company and Bank of America Corporation.[7] The covenant specifies that Qwest's debt be less than four times ebitda (earnings before interest, taxes, depreciation, and amortization.) The current estimate of ebitda for 2002 is $5.4 billion to $5.6 billion. The company currently has $26.6 billion in debt. The company is working to amend the debt covenant to avoid having the $4 billion become due immediately.

Questions

a. Identify the interested parties involved in this pattern of transactions. Who benefits by the revenue recognition policy used by Qwest? Is anyone harmed if telecommunications companies recognize revenue based on round-trip trades?

b. Based on your knowledge of GAAP principles and the concept statements on the quality of information provided by financial reports, criticize the revenue recognition policy justified by Arthur Andersen in the "white paper." What accounting concepts did Andersen violate in their recommendation?

c. Based on your knowledge of GAAP principles and the concept statements on the quality of information provided by financial reports, support or criticize the revenue recognition decision by the SEC.

d. Given the importance of revenue as a measure of a company's health, does recording revenue based on round-trip trades give outside users of financial statements a good measure of the company's health?

e. If company executives received stock options based on performance, how might this have influenced their choice of accounting method for revenue recognition? Explain. Show your reasoning.

f. Do you think the banks should amend the debt covenants? Would you support such change? (As a banker? As a shareholder? As a company accountant?)

g. Do you believe that company executives engaged in fraudulent activity by their use of round-trip transactions to increase revenue? Do you think they should be shielded from liability for earlier transactions because the SEC only recently issued a formal statement that telecommunications companies could not recognize revenue for round-trip transactions? Explain your answer.

h. Stock prices dropped after the restatements were announced. Why might this action have had such a result?

i. Which alternative of revenue recognition best represents the economic situation of Qwest—following the Andersen "white paper" advice or the later SEC "suggestion"? Discuss in detail.

Case 2.2
Bristol-Myers Squibb

Bristol-Myers produces and distributes medicines and healthcare products. In 2002, the company experienced one of its worst years in its 100-year history. Three of its top-selling drugs lost patent protection, and sales dramatically declined due to generic substitutes produced by other companies. The share price of Bristol-Myers stock declined by nearly two-thirds (from about $75 in September 1999 to $25 in September 2002).

In April 2002, the company disclosed that it had used sales incentives to encourage wholesalers to buy more drugs and healthcare products than necessary. In July 2002, Bristol-Myers was notified that the SEC was opening a formal inquiry to determine whether the company had inflated revenue by as much as $1 billion in 2001 through the use of sales incentives.[8] The company consequently restated the amount of the excessive sales three times. In August 2002, the company estimated the excessive wholesale purchases to be about $1.5 billion in sales.[9] As a result of the restatement and the declining sales, company officials projected that 2002 earnings would be only half that of 2001.

Bristol-Myers management claimed that its accounting treatment was appropriate. The company is cooperating fully with the ongoing SEC investigation.

Questions

a. What is the ethical dilemma described in this scenario?
b. Identify the interested parties in the transactions. Who benefits from the inflated report of revenue? Who does this form of revenue recognition harm?
c. Noting the declining sales, what role might this have played in Bristol-Myers' decision to provide sales incentives to its customers?

Case 2.3
Computer Associates International, Inc.

Computer Associates is a New York–based software company that creates networking programs for its corporate clients.[10] Financial information for the company follows.[11]

Year	Revenue (in billions)	Net Income (in millions)
1997	$3.0	$ 366
1998	$4.2	$ 1,200
1999	$4.7	$ 624
2000	$6.1	$ 656
2001	$4.2	$ 591
2002	$3.0	$ (1,100)

When the company appeared to be growing faster than its competitors, increasing revenue led to stock price increases. In May 1998, the stock price reached $55.13. This triggered a special stock incentive award to the top three executives of the firm. The stock grant was worth roughly $1 billion and was paid to Charles Wang, then its chief executive officer; President Sanjay Kumar; and Russell Artz, the head of research. The SEC is investigating the company's overstatement of revenue in 1998 and 1999, before and after the stock grants.

SEC investigators are also determining whether company executives manipulated revenue from software license leases to report higher revenue.[12] Investigators think Computer Associates may have recorded software-licensing revenue for long-term contracts before it received the money, despite the fact that many of these contracts were cancelled before they expired or were replaced by contracts of lesser value.

Shortly after the $1 billion in stock awards were paid to the top executives, the company began retroactively adjusting its revenue downward, referring to the adjustments as reclassifications and not restatements. (The revenue removed was offset by a reduction in expense with no effect on net income.)[13] The revenue revisions appear to have been prompted by a switch in auditors from Ernst and Young to KPMG in June 1999. According to a statement issued by Computer Associates, the company intends to "defend against unwarranted allegations in court" (regarding the stock awards). The company's outside lawyers have described the top executives, Wang and Kumar, as "arms-length" managers who only casually reviewed regulatory filings such as 10K and 10Q annual and quarterly reports, and left the complex details of licensing accounting for subordinates in the finance department. The stock price rose to a high of $70 in 2000.

At the annual meeting in August 2002, Computer Associates announced several replacements on the board of directors.[14] Eight of the eleven directors are now outsiders. At the meeting, several shareholders questioned executives and expressed anger over their use of the corporate jets for vacation travel and attendance at games of the New York Islanders hockey team, which Wang and Kumar own. By September 2002, Computer Associates' stock dropped to $9.98.

Questions

a.   What is the ethical dilemma suggested by the revenue recognition in this situation? What do the published reports have to do with stock prices?

b. The executive officers benefited from the revenue reports. Who, if anyone, was harmed? Were any outsiders to the company harmed?

c. Why would the SEC launch an investigation of the internal matter of stock grants at Computer Associates? Isn't it the company's own business as to how it awards its executive officers?

d. Did the revenue reports fairly represent the economic situation of the company?

e. Are the company's adjustments as reclassifications an adequate accounting practice?

f. What responsibility, if any, does the original auditor, Ernest and Young, bear for the misleading statements in the annual reports? Has the audit firm acted in an unethical manner? Explain your answer.

Case 2.4
AOL Time Warner

In July 2002, the SEC reviewed revenue transactions by the America Online unit of AOL Time Warner to determine whether the company used "unconventional" ad deals to increase revenue to meet expectations of Wall Street analysts. In addition, the U.S. Justice Department initiated a criminal investigation into the company's revenue recognition procedures in the Internet division.

An article appearing in *The Washington Post* on July 18, 2002, alleged that AOL manipulated its ad revenue at a time when it was waiting for approval of the Time Warner merger. The company owns CNN cable news, HBO, Warner Brothers, and *Time* magazine, in addition to the AOL Internet division, and was formed by a merger between AOL and Time Warner on January 21, 2001.[15] AOL's revenue for 2001 was $38.2 billion and net income was $(4.9) billion.

A Washington Post reporter reviewed a number of AOL's revenue transactions from July 2000 to March 2002. Without the "unconventional" deals described in the article, quarterly earnings per share would not have met analysts' forecasts for two quarters in 2000. According to the *Post*, during this time, "investors punished companies whose earnings were off by even a cent."[16]

AOL employees interviewed for the article said that the company was under tremendous pressure to meet its revenue targets due to the $112 billion acquisition of Time Warner. Ad revenue became very important to the Internet division as competition from other Internet service providers hurt AOL's monthly subscriber fees. Unfortunately, the contracts for the advertising services were with dot-com companies, which also were suffering from declining sales. Many of the dot-com companies did not have the cash to pay for the ads they had agreed to buy with AOL.

The business affairs department of the Internet division of AOL was responsible for improving ad revenue. This unit was referred to as "the BA unit" and their ad deals were referred to as "BA Specials," a reference to the aggressive methods used by the department to generate ad revenue. The "unconventional" deals include a variety of methods to increase revenue. The business affairs department contacted companies with long-term ad contracts that they were unable to pay and renegotiated the terms of the agreements, requiring the companies to make one-time payments to renegotiate or get out of the contracts. AOL would recognize all the revenue for the renegotiated contracts immediately as ad revenue. From July 2000 to March 2001, AOL recorded $56 million from contracts that were terminated or restructured.

Earlier, in September 2000, AOL used another "unconventional" ad deal to generate revenue. It recorded ad revenue based on a lawsuit settlement. AOL purchased Movie Fone in 1999, and Movie Fone had won a $26.8 million settlement claim that had not yet been collected from Wembley PLC, a British entertainment company. Instead of collecting the settlement, AOL offered Wembley the opportunity to buy $23.8 million in online ads (a good deal for Wembley since they save $3 million). AOL was short of advertising revenue for the quarter ending on September 30, 2000, so the ads had to be created and aired before the end of the quarter.

Wembley considered the proposal for some time, but AOL could not wait for its decision because the ad revenue had to be booked in September 2000. Without Wembley's knowledge, AOL took artwork off Wembley's British website (24 Dogs.com, an online greyhound racing website) and created banner and button ads of the artwork and started running them on various AOL sites. Within an hour of posting the greyhound ads, the Wembley website crashed, due to the traffic generated by the AOL ads.

Wembley and AOL reached an ad agreement despite AOL's action. This ad agreement generated $16.4 million in ad revenue for the September 30, 2000, quarter, effectively taking a nonoperating gain on a lawsuit settlement (when it was paid) and converting it to a more valuable operating revenue number.

In July 2001, AOL found a new source for ad revenue. AOL signed an agreement with eBay to serve as its ad broker. This involved selling the ad space on the eBay website. Instead of recognizing the commission revenue from this arrangement, AOL recorded the entire revenue from the eBay advertisements, taking an expense for the payments it sent to eBay. This arrangement had no impact on AOL's net income, but it allowed AOL to record a larger amount for ad revenue. AOL recorded $80 million in revenue for 2000 and 2001 from the eBay arrangement.

Under accounting standards, it might have been appropriate for AOL to record the gross revenue if AOL assumed a financial risk in this transaction. Because AOL was not obligated to pay eBay if the advertiser did not pay the bill, AOL did not have a financial risk in the transaction.

In January 2002, AOL Time Warner made history when it took a $54.2 billion pre-tax charge to write down the value of goodwill from the acquisition of Time Warner, making it the largest write-off of goodwill assets.[17] The first quarter goodwill adjustment did not include a reduction for the goodwill on the America Online Internet Service unit. AOL's online division had been suffering from declining ad revenue, a small growth in subscriber sales, and criminal and civil investigations into its accounting practices. Considering these factors, it is likely that the division has suffered a decline in fair value—a condition requiring a write-down of goodwill in the division. The market value of AOL's stock is $60.4 billion. Without the $125.1 billion of intangible assets, including $80.1 billion of goodwill, AOL would have a negative book value.

Questions

a. Identify the parties affected by the company's use of "unconventional" ad deals. Who benefits? Who was harmed?

b. What is the ethical dilemma in this situation? Can you resolve the dilemma by referring to the accounting rules on revenue recognition? Did AOL recognize revenue according to GAAP?

c. Discuss the role the planned AOL Time Warner merger played in the decisions regarding the "unconventional" ad deals.

d. Evaluate the information disclosed to outsiders in terms of relevance, reliability, and bias.

e. Did the "unconventional" ad revenue represent the underlying economic reality of the transaction?

Case 2.5
Xerox Corporation

Xerox Corporation, a company based in Stamford, Connecticut, is involved in the production and management of documents in the form of copy machines, fax machines, and commercial printing equipment. In the late 1990s, competition had a negative impact on Xerox sales (among other things, computer printers were replacing copiers to generate print copies). A poorly organized business restructuring also caused administrative problems and billing and sales slowdowns. The accounting department at Xerox began getting pressure to compensate for the poor sales results with accounting measures. Xerox "assigned accountants numerical goals to produce profits through accounting actions. It just became standard operating procedure that, you know, you look to the accountants to find income." [18]

Following an SEC settlement with Xerox, the FBI opened an inquiry into the possibility of filing criminal charges against the individuals involved in the earnings misstatement that led to the restatement of Xerox earnings earlier in 2002.[19] In April 2002, Xerox had settled a case with the SEC, agreeing to pay a $10 million fine and restating its results back to 1997. Xerox neither admitted nor denied any wrongdoing in the settlement. The restatement showed that it had recorded $6.4 billion of revenue early and had overstated its pretax income by $1.41 billion over the five years, a 36 percent overstatement. Financial information for the company follows.

Year	Revenue (in billions)	Net Income (in billions)
1997	$18.1	$ 1.4
1998	$19.6	$ 0.4
1999	$19.0	$ 0.8
2000	$18.8	$ (0.3)
2001	$17.0	$ (0.1)

The stock price was above $40 per share (up to a high of about $62) in 1998 and 1999. In 2000, the stock price dropped to about $20 per share, and in 2002 the price dropped to less than $10 per share ($6.60 in September 2002.)[20]

Paul R. Berger, Associate Director of Enforcement at the SEC, described the actions of Xerox executives in the enforcement notice: "Xerox's senior management orchestrated a four-year scheme to disguise the company's true operating performance. Such conduct calls for stiff sanctions, including in this case, the imposition of the largest fine ever obtained by the SEC against a public company in a financial fraud case. The penalty also reflects, in part, a sanction for the company's lack of full cooperation in the investigation."[21]

The SEC enforcement notice reported that the company recorded long-term leasing agreements for copiers over shorter periods than the leases ran, in order to record more revenue during the early years of the leases. The company also made a one-time sale of accounts receivable to increase operating results but failed to disclose this fact to outsiders. Xerox established a "cookie jar" reserve account that was set up to cover merger costs, but instead was used to meet analysts' quarterly earnings forecasts. From 1997 to 2000, the SEC alleged that senior managers at Xerox were paid over $5 million on performance-based compensation. They also made more than $30 million from the sale of company stock.

In a related SEC inquiry, notices of possible civil action for fraud were sent to KPMG, Xerox's former auditor (they were fired in 2001), and a number of Xerox executives (both current and former employees). KPMG said it did nothing wrong in its work for Xerox and was, in fact, fired for forcing Xerox to conduct an independent accounting exam that resulted in an earlier Xerox restatement. The restatement in 2001 prompted the SEC investigation in 2002. The SEC has also said that it is considering forcing Xerox executives to return the performance-based compensation they wrongfully obtained during the restated years. Xerox executives are likely to argue that they relied upon the accounting guidance provided by KPMG.

The scandal came to the attention of the SEC because of a wrongful termination case brought by a fired Xerox employee, James Bingham. Bingham filed a lawsuit alleging that he was fired by Xerox in 2000 after he questioned their accounting practices. Bingham became an important witness in the SEC investigation of Xerox and is expected to continue in this role in the civil fraud investigation against company executives.

Bingham described a transaction designed to increase sales revenue. In 1999, Xerox recorded short-term rental agreements for copiers in Brazil and elsewhere as if they were long-term leases. This allowed Xerox to immediately record the future rental revenue. Bingham told the SEC investigators that the arrangements were recorded in this manner to help the company meet analysts' forecasts. Bingham told the SEC that Xerox executives knew the company was in trouble. Bingham said that Leslie Varon, Xerox's investor-relations chief, warned him in early 1999 to get rid of his stock options because the company was "falling apart at the seams."

The public first became aware of the trouble at Xerox in May 2000, when the company announced it had found "serious accounting irregularities" in Mexico, and the SEC began to investigate these irregularities. Bingham said that he had been involved in discussions with the director of worldwide audits at Xerox during the SEC investigation in Mexico, where they "discussed more than $500 million in special accounting actions in 1998 and 1999, and Xerox's need to do everything it could to keep the investigation in Mexico."[22]

A few weeks after the Mexican accounting scandal broke, Bingham sent a memo to Anne Mulcahy, company president, and Barry Romeril, chief financial officer. In the memo, he described some of his accounting concerns. Bingham was invited to give a presentation describing his concerns to Romeril and two other senior executives. In this presentation, he sharply criticized the accounting practices and the corporate culture at Xerox. He said it was a "high likelihood" that Xerox had issued "misleading financial statements and public disclosures." Two days later, he was fired.

Recent events have demonstrated that many of his allegations were true. After months of denying Bingham's allegations, Xerox restated its results for 1997–2000 and acknowledged that it had misapplied accounting rules in a variety of ways.

Questions

a. Identify the parties involved in the earnings manipulation of Xerox. Who benefited from the increased revenue? Was anyone harmed?

b. Describe the role of the financial analysts in the earnings manipulation. Why is their position important, even though they do not work for Xerox?

c. The stock price was likely to have been influenced by the reports of accounting irregularities. What happened to stock prices? Explain this impact.

d. Is KMPG likely to avoid liability for the earnings manipulations? What role might the auditors have played in this situation? If you were a KMPG auditor team examining Xerox, what might you have said and/or done?

e. Evaluate the actions of James Bingham. What pressures were brought to bear on him as he attempted to act responsibly? Did he fulfill his professional duties? Should he have testified against his company?

f. Xerox made a number of restatements. Given your knowledge of the situation, was the remedy of restatements an adequate response? If you were a shareholder in Xerox, what might you think of the executives' actions?

g. Does the board of directors share any responsibility for the executives' actions? What might a board have done to protect the company from its management's actions?

h. Given these circumstances, are there any good reasons for a company to have performance-based incentives that are connected with earnings? How else might performance be measured?

Case 2.6
Global Crossing, Ltd.

Global Crossing, a company registered in Bermuda, was formed in 1997 by Gary Winnick. At one time, the value of Global Crossing's network of fiber-optic cables was greater than the value of General Motors.[23] However, in January 2002, Global Crossing (GC) filed for bankruptcy protection (at that time, the fourth largest bankruptcy filing in history). In August 2002, GC was purchased for $250 million by a pair of Asian conglomerates. The purchase price was just over 1 percent of its bankruptcy-reported value of $22 billion.

In May 2002, the SEC interviewed GC executives to determine if sales transactions made by the company in 2001 were designed solely to increase revenue.[24] Roy Olofson, a former Global Crossing financial executive, alleged that transactions where GC swapped telecommunication capacity with other carriers had "little economic substance and were only used to inflate the company's 2001 revenue." These swap transactions involved hundreds of millions of dollars.[25]

The revenue transactions also came under scrutiny by the U.S. House Energy and Commerce Committee.[26] The House Committee spent seven months in 2002 investigating the widespread practice in the telecommunications industry of "swapping" fiber-optic capacity. Under such arrangements, companies such as Qwest, Global Crossing, and Cable and Wireless PLC exchanged equal amounts of telecom capacity. Each company recognized revenue for the exchanges and recorded the cost of providing the capacity as a capital expense.

Witnesses before the House Energy Panel described the business environment in the telecom industry in 2001 as a "pressure cooker." During this period, the executives at the top of companies pushed their sales representatives at lower levels to meet the companies' quarterly sales targets. According to Patrick Joggerst, former head of carrier sales at Global Crossing, "Not meeting the numbers was absolutely unacceptable."[27] To meet the revenue targets, sales representatives from one company called their counterparts at other companies and worked out swap transactions that helped the companies meet their sales targets. In 2001, Global Crossing purchased $1.2 billion in capacity from companies where it sold $1.0 billion in capacity. Robin Szeliga, Qwest's chief financial officer, testified that "there were well known consequences for not making the numbers but no clear consequences for cutting corners."[28]

Investigators also reviewed the stock transactions for company executives, including founder Gary Winnick. In May 2001, during the period where swap transactions were used to inflate revenues, Winnick sold $123 million in Global Crossing stock.

In August 2002, the SEC issued an opinion that the recognition related to the swap transactions was not recorded properly and that companies that used such transactions would have to restate their earnings. Qwest agreed to restate $1.1 billion in revenue related to the swap transactions.[29] However, Global Crossing did not agree to a restatement.

Questions

a. Identify the accounting problem described in this scenario.
b. What accounting principle or concepts do you think was used to justify Global Crossing's treatment of the swap transactions?
c. What accounting principles or concepts did Global Crossing violate?
d. Evaluate the revenue information provided to outside users when a company increases revenue through the use of swap transactions. Is the information relevant or reliable? Does the information represent the underlying economic reality of the transaction?
e. Identify the parties who were affected by the revenue recognition policy. Who benefits? Who is harmed?
f. What role may the pressure from top executives of these telecom companies have played in the revenue recognition policy? Is this policy of revenue recognition an appropriate method? What should the accountants in these firms have done?

Case 2.7
Merck-Medco

Between 1999 and 2001, Merck-Medco, the nation's second largest pharmacy-benefits manager, recorded $12.4 billion in revenue that it will never collect.[30] Merck's Medco unit included as part of revenue the co-payments collected by pharmacies from patients, even though Medco does not receive these funds. For the three-year period, the co-payments accounted for nearly 10 percent of Merck's total revenue.

Merck first disclosed the revenue recognition policy in an April 2002 SEC filing in preparation for selling 20 percent of Medco in an initial public offering (IPO). Merck maintains that the revenue recognition is consistent with GAAP. The company says the accounting choice has no impact on net income because the company subtracts the same amount as an expense.

The $12.4 billion in revenue is paid directly to the pharmacies by consumers using a prescription drug card to cover their portion of the prescription cost under an insurance plan. The co-payment is typically $10–$15 per prescription. The pharmacies keep the entire co-payment, but Medco records the co-payment as revenue, despite the fact that Medco does not bill the co-payment or come into contact with it.

Medco, handles the pharmacy benefits of 65 million Americans. Advance PCS, the country's largest PBM, and Express Scripts, the third-largest pharmacy-benefits manager, do not include co-payments as part of their revenue. By contrast, Caremark RX, the fourth largest company, does include co-payments as part of revenue. Arthur Andersen audited the books of Caremark, Advance PCS, and Merck-Medco until 2002. PricewaterhouseCoopers audits the books for Express Scripts.

After an article published in *The Wall Street Journal* disclosed Merck's revenue recognition policy, Merck's stock price dropped 5 percent to a five-year low. After the disclosure, at least four shareholder lawsuits were filed alleging the company falsely inflated its revenue by treating prescription co-payments as revenue.

Questions

a. Is Merck-Medco's revenue recognition policy consistent with GAAP? Explain your answer.

b. The SEC has begun a crackdown on business practices that falsely inflate revenue. How might the SEC criticize the revenue recognition policies of Merck?

c. Is Merck's revenue recognition policy consistent with the underlying economic reality of the transaction?

d. Evaluate the quality of the revenue number given to outsiders. Is the information relevant and reliable?

e. Identify the interested parties in this accounting decision. Who benefits? Who is harmed?

f. Arthur Andersen was the auditor for three of the four largest pharmacy benefits managers. Why did one Andersen audit client not recognize co-payments as revenue while the other two did recognize co-payments as revenue? (That is, what might each company gain with its revenue recognition policy?) It seems reasonable to expect similar revenue practices in an industry. If so, should Andersen have advised its clients to recognize revenue in one particular way? Which form of disclosure do you recommend? Explain your answer.

Case 2.8
Mirant Corporation

Mirant Corporation, an Atlanta-based energy company, was investigated in 2002 by the SEC for round-trip trading activities and $250 million in accounting irregularities.[31] In addition to the SEC investigation, the Federal Energy Regulatory Commission examined energy-trading practices in the western United States, including how energy companies may have manipulated the market during California's energy crisis in 2000 and 2001 to create power shortages and drive up gas prices.

Several energy companies, including Mirant, Dynegy, Duke Energy, and El Paso, received subpoenas from the SEC, the U.S. Justice Department, and from the Commodity Futures Trading Commission over their trading and accounting policies. These companies entered into round-trip trading using swap accounting where two companies enter into a trade of the same amount of energy for the same price. The trades are used to inflate revenue, although from an economic perspective neither company has changed its economic situation through the transaction. Round-trip trading seems to serve no economic purpose other than inflating revenue.

A Mirant spokesperson said, "We will cooperate fully with this request for information. Transparency has, and always will be, a cornerstone of Mirant's code of conduct."[32] After the announcement of the investigation, Mirant's stock price fell 16 percent to $2.93.

Questions

a.   Is revenue recognition based on round-trip energy sales consistent with GAAP?
b.   Identify the parties interested in this transaction. Who benefits? Who is harmed?
c.   What does the company spokesperson mean when he says, "Transparency has, and always will be, a cornerstone of Mirant's code of conduct?" Does transparency improve financial disclosure?
d.   Why do you think the stock price of Mirant stock declined 16 percent after the announcement of the investigation?
e.   If you were the company accountant at Mirant or the auditor for the company, would you support the use of round-trip accounting? Explain your reasons.

Case 2.9
Revenue Recognition for Unearned Revenue

Susan Webb is reviewing the journal entries made by the accounting staff at *The Daily Press*. As controller of the company, her job is to make sure that the financial statements are accurate at the end of the month. She has received congratulations from the president of the company related to the preliminary revenue numbers for July. To her dismay, she discovers that the July numbers appear to be incorrect. Several new accountants have been recording unearned revenue subscriptions as earned revenue. She knows that the president plans to have a staff meeting tomorrow to congratulate the staff for the increase in revenue. She wonders whether she should speak with the president before the meeting.

Questions

a.   What is the ethical dilemma described in this problem?
b.   Discuss the accounting issue presented by this dilemma.
c.   What alternatives are available to Susan? (Consider timeliness as a factor.)
d.   Identify the interested parties in this decision. Who benefits? Who is harmed?

e. Based on your knowledge of generally accepted accounting principles, how would you resolve this dilemma?

Case 2.10
Allowance for Sales Returns

Arctic Cat Manufacturing is preparing its year-end financial statements in late December. Audrey Brooks, the controller of Arctic Cat, has heard that the unusually dry winter has prompted a large number of returns of snowmobiles to the company. She wants to take a conservative approach and reduce sales revenue by an estimate of future returns. Her supervisor, Sharon Johnson, prefers to record sales at the highest level, possibly arguing that it is too early in the winter to predict the rate of returns.

Questions

a. Assume that Audrey estimates the returns to be $3 million, while her supervisor's estimate is $500,000. Based on your knowledge of GAAP, evaluate the two alternatives presented in this problem. Does GAAP tell you whether Audrey or Sharon is correct?

b. Identify the interested parties in this situation. Who benefits? Who is harmed?

c. What would you do in this situation? Justify your answer.

Case 2.11
Accelerating Sales Revenue

In order to increase revenue at the end of the year, Publishers, Inc., a distributor of books and magazines, offers its customers the opportunity to purchase books and magazines at a 35 percent discount, if they increase their purchases by 25 percent over the prior month. Marcia Quincy, the controller, complains to the financial vice president, Andy Banes, that recording revenue in this fashion will hurt the company in the future; plus it may result in a great deal of work when the excess stock is returned. Andy replies that this policy is the only way the company can increase its net income to obtain a short-term loan at the bank. Andy adds: "What difference does it make if we encourage our customers to purchase inventory items a little early, even if they return them? The sales will come in the future. Besides, by the time they return the inventory, we'll have the loan and it won't make a difference if net income is lower next year."

Questions

a. Answer Andy's question, "What difference does it make?" Based on your knowledge of GAAP, does it make a difference if the sales are recorded this year or next? Is either method acceptable in this circumstance?

b. Is the discount program a reasonable way to increase revenue?
c. What moral dilemma does Marcia recognize? Who is harmed by the discount program? Who benefits from the program?
d. Does GAAP allow you to solve this ethical dilemma?
e. If Marcia decides to argue vigorously against the discount policy, how might she make her argument?
f. What would you do?

Case 2.12
Sales Revenue

The treasurer and the controller for Steen College are discussing ways to generate revenue for the next school year. Student enrollment has declined during the past three years. Unless enrollment increases in the college during the next school year, the officials will need to reduce the number of teachers on the payroll. Linda White, the treasurer, says that she has a great idea based on a recent article in *The Wall Street Journal*. This article reported that many colleges and universities inflate the test scores and graduation rates in popular college guidebooks. For example, New College of the University of Southern Florida was ranked number 1 in *Money* magazine's 2004 College Guide. The average SAT score of 1296 for the freshmen class placed this school among the most selective in the country. But the score was false. For years New College deliberately inflated its SAT scores by 40 points by dropping the bottom 6 percent of student scores from the calculation. The admissions director described this practice as part of the college's marketing strategy. The director admitted that the practice raised some ethical questions, but he stated that other schools also report false numbers. The article reports many examples of excluding certain groups from the statistics reported for the purpose of improving the college's reputation. In some instances, the numbers were completely fabricated to make the school look good. Many of the same colleges that report false information to the numerous guidebook companies also report accurate information to debt-rating agencies such as Moody's, as required when these institutions sell bonds or debt instruments. Why do these colleges take this contradictory approach? Reporting false information to debt-rating agencies violates federal securities laws, but reporting false information to guidebook publishers results in no legal penalties.[33]

Questions

a. What is the ethical dilemma described in this problem?
b. Discuss the marketing strategy of New College. Is this strategy ethical? Who benefits? Who is harmed by this strategy?
c. The admissions director of New College admitted that the policy of lying to companies that compile guidebooks raised some ethical questions, but he rationalized that because everyone was doing it, it was acceptable. Comment on this conclusion.

d. Why are colleges reporting inaccurate information for use in guidebooks, but providing debt-rating agencies with accurate information? Is it ethical to report accurate financial information only when you are forced to by legal penalties?

e. The controller for Steen College has been accurately reporting information to both the guidebook companies and the debt-rating agencies. He is not sure he wants to follow the trend toward inaccurate reporting, but he is not anxious to fire any teachers, since many of them are his close friends. What alternatives are available to him?

f. What would you do?

g. Based on your experiences in selecting schools, was your school accurately described in guidebooks? Does it make a difference to you if your institution provides inaccurate information to publishing companies for college guidebooks?

Case 2.13
Collecting Contributions

As controller of Pacific University, you have just received a letter from Walt Peterson, bankruptcy trustee of the New. Wealth Foundation. New Wealth, a charity that had promised to double contributors' money within six months, has been sued for fraudulent activity and has filed for bankruptcy protection. You had considered yourself lucky to be one of the 75 institutions to come out ahead in your dealings with New Wealth. Pacific University had contributed $300,000 to the New Wealth Foundation and within six months had doubled its money to $600,000. Many other creditors lost their entire contribution. The bankruptcy judge has requested that you repay the $300,000, so it can be used to cover the losses for individuals who deposited money and lost their investments (75 creditors gained $21.6 million; 225 creditors lost $107 million). You have a great deal of sympathy for the not-for-profit institutions who lost money, but you have already spent the $300,000 on renovations to the business building on campus, and you do not want to replace the money. You wonder if you are obligated to return the money as the bankruptcy judge has requested.

Questions

a. What is the ethical dilemma described in this problem?
b. Identify the parties affected by this decision. Who benefits? Who is harmed?
c. What alternatives are available to the controller?
d. What would you do? Why?

Case 2.14
Revenue Recognition for Installment Sales

Jane Wagner and Justin Stine are reviewing the accounting rules for recording an installment sale. Jane and Justin work in the plastics division of their company, which has been under pressure to improve earnings. Their division has just made a large installment sale, and they want to record it in a fashion that makes the division look better. The total revenue generated as a result of the installment sale is $15 million, to be paid in five yearly installments of $3 million. Normally the division does not use installment sales to generate income, but in this instance they believed it was justified given the size of the sale and the potential benefit to the division. Jane says that they should recognize all the revenue in year one, because this will help the division meet its sales quota and assure that management receives favorable evaluations and salary increases. Justin doesn't believe it appropriate to recognize all the revenue in year one for installment sales. He argues that they should recognize gross profit as the cash is received. Jane says: "We can get by with recording all the revenue in the first year and setting up a note receivable for the balance due. Management will think we are acting correctly because they will not recognize that an installment sale is different from other types of sales. Besides, this is just a 'normal' sale with credit terms of five years, and not much different than those sales with the normal credit terms of 60 days."

Questions

a. What is the accounting issue involved in the recording of the installment sale?
b. Identify the interested parties involved in this situation. Who benefits? Who is harmed?
c. What is the ethical dilemma described in the problem?
d. Identify several alternatives available to Justin.
e. Based on your knowledge of GAAP, what should Justin do? Why?
f. What would you do? Explain your answer to Jane.

Case 2.15
Obsolete Inventory

John Harris and Susan Ernest are discussing the inventory obsolescence policy for Smith Communications, a manufacturer of satellite dishes used for communication purposes. Since changes in technology make inventory parts obsolete very quickly, obsolescent inventory is a major problem. John has a suggestion for reducing the dollar amounts on the obsolete information report, and he is discussing this idea with Susan, his supervisor. Last year the auditors ran a computerized report of all inventory items having no activity in the last twelve months. Several thousand dollars worth of inventory appeared on this report. This year, expecting that the auditors will run a similar report, John has suggested to Susan that they make it appear that all the inventory has moved by transferring parts from one location to another, thus making it look like the items are still being used. John says: "The auditors will never catch this transfer. They are not smart enough to consider the way we moved this inventory. They will simply run their computer reports, and if the report tells them that the part number was used in the last twelve months, they do not consider how it was used. It will be important for us to start this process about six months before year-end and to complete it a couple of months before the auditors arrive. I think it will work just fine. We used to get auditors that would think, but now they are so fascinated by computers that they sometimes fail to realize what they're doing."

Questions

a. What is the ethical dilemma described in this problem?
b. Identify the parties affected by this decision. Who benefits? Who is harmed?
c. Evaluate John's statement that auditors are so fascinated by computers that they fail to think about what they're doing. Do you agree with the statement?
d. What alternatives are available to John and Susan?
e. Do you believe John should be making this proposal to his supervisor, Susan?
f. If you were John's boss, what would you tell him?
g. What decision would you make in this situation? Why?

Case 2.16
Matching Expenses to Revenue

Andrea's new accounting supervisor, Kathryn Baldwin, is very demanding and wants everything done perfectly. She reviews the supplies account for St. John's College and wants to know why Andrea is expensing the computers purchased this year. She says, "Don't you know that computers should be depreciated over three years? Your behavior is unethical. You should never expense equipment that can be used for more than one year. Didn't you learn anything in school? The only way a company can prepare an accurate income statement is to match expenses with revenues. If you take all the expense for the computers in year one, but use these computers for three years, you are not matching revenues and expenses. I can't believe you would engage in this type of unethical behavior."

Questions

a. How should Andrea respond?
b. Is Andrea acting unethically? Should she change her procedure for expensing computers?
c. How should Andrea explain her decision to Kathryn?

Net Profit Versus Gross Profit

Forrest Gump, one of the most profitable movies released by Paramount Pictures in 1994, lost $62 million dollars, despite box office sales of more than $657 million, due to creative accounting measures used by Paramount Pictures to calculate net income. Paramount Pictures achieved this loss by allocating distribution expenses to this movie to wipe out the profit generated by a successful product. The losers in this process were Winston Groom, the author who created the Forrest Gump character, and Eric Roth, the screenwriter. Both men were promised a percentage of the net profits. Since there were no net profits, they were paid only the amounts of the original contract. Tom Hanks, the actor who portrayed Forrest Gump in the movie, and Robert Zemeckis, the director, signed contracts promising them 8 percent of the gross profits of the movie, so their contracts have been enriched by the box office success of the movie.[34]

Questions

a. What is the difference between net profit and gross profit? Do you think that Winston Groom understands this difference now?
b. If you were an accountant at Paramount Pictures, would you use your accounting knowledge to take advantage of individuals like Winston Groom and Eric Roth? Explain your answer.
c. Are the stockholders in the company harmed by this decision? Explain your answer.

EXPENSE RECOGNITION

Case 2.18
WorldCom, Inc.

In 2002, WorldCom, Inc., a telecommunications company based in Clinton, Mississippi, was one of the world's largest telecommunications companies, with 20 million customers, thousands of corporate clients, and 62,000 employees.[35] Financial information for the company follows.

Year	Revenue (in billions)	Net Income (in billions)
1999	$19.7	$2.6
2000	$22.8	$3.0
2001	$21.3	$1.5

Earnings Restatements

However, in June 2002, WorldCom announced a $3.8 billion earnings restatement due to expenses that had been improperly recorded as capital expenditures. By July 1, the stock had dropped to $.05 from a high of $64.50 in June 1999.[36] WorldCom filed for bankruptcy shortly thereafter.

The SEC issued the following response to the WorldCom bankruptcy announcement: "The WorldCom disclosures confirm that accounting improprieties of unprecedented magnitude have been committed in the public markets."[37] The restatement turned the previously reported profit numbers for 2001 ($1.4 billion) and the first quarter of 2002 ($130 million) into losses.

The accounting errors were discovered during a routine investigation by the internal audit department at WorldCom. The information was turned over to the board of directors' audit committee and to the independent auditor, KPMG, which had replaced Arthur Andersen as auditors in May 2002. After the investigation, WorldCom issued a statement announcing the accounting improprieties, "certain transfers from line cost expenses to capital assets," were not made in accordance with GAAP. The total amount of the transfers was $3.8 billion for the four quarters of 2001 and the first quarter of 2002.

In August 2002, WorldCom revised the amount of the earnings restatement from $3.8 billion to $7.2 billion.[38] WorldCom warned that it would have to revise its earning for 2000, in addition to the 2001 and 2002 restatements. The 2000 restatement is related to a time period when insiders were selling company stock. For example, former WorldCom chief financial officer, Scott Sullivan, sold shares valued at $18.1 million during 2000. The new restatement reduced the 2000 net income to a net loss. In this disclosure, the company also warned that it could be forced to take a $50 billion goodwill write-off. The $3.2 billion restatement in August 2002 was related to several accounting errors including overstatement of revenue, improper capitalizing of expenses, plus cookie-jar reserve reversals (funds set aside to cover future expenses, which are reversed as needed to increase revenue). Regulators were concerned that companies wrongly set up reserve accounts and then reversed out the reserves when revenues fell short of Wall Street analysts' expectations.

In September 2002, WorldCom announced a further restatement of about $2 billion, to be added to the $7 billion total, making the "largest accounting fraud ever" even bigger. The new restatement was said to be related "in part to the company's accounting for the results of a foreign subsidiary." WorldCom appears to have consolidated the results of one of its subsidiaries, Embrated Participacoes SA, when it was profitable (contributing 8.6 percent of WorldCom's revenues in 2000) and not consolidating results when it was unprofitable.[39]

Company Executives

Scott Sullivan, former chief financial officer, and Buford "Buddy" Yates, Jr., a former accounting executive, were charged with securities fraud, conspiring to commit securities fraud, and making false filings to the SEC, and were indicted by a federal grand jury in August 2002.[40] Two other accounting executives who worked for Yates were named as unindicted co-conspirators. Betty Vinson and Troy Normand waived indictment and are cooperating with investigators. In September 2002, David F. Myers, the former controller of WorldCom, pleaded guilty to three felony counts, saying he helped manufacture profits at the request of senior management as part of an attempt by management to defraud investors and meet Wall Street expectations. At the court hearing, Myers said he was "instructed on a quarterly basis by senior management to ensure that entries were made to falsify WorldCom's books, to reduce WorldCom's reported actual costs and thereby increase WorldCom's reported earnings." Myers told the court that he made the entries even though he "knew there was no justification or documentation."[41]

The U.S. House Energy and Commerce Committee also investigated the accounting practices of WorldCom. The committee released documents gathered during the investigation that showed WorldCom employees had tried to question the accounting practices but were told to keep quiet. A WorldCom executive also notified Arthur Andersen, the company's auditor, more than two years prior that the company was inflating net income but the practice of recording expense as capital assets continued.[42]

The documents released provide detail about Steven Brabbs, a London-based WorldCom executive responsible for Europe and Asia. In March 2000, Brabbs questioned a $33.6 million reduction in expense for his division. This charge made his profit numbers look better than they were. When Brabbs questioned corporate headquarters about the entry, he was told it was made "because of a directive from Sullivan" (the chief financial officer). When Brabbs persisted in following up on the directive by sending a letter to Arthur Andersen and senior financial executives at WorldCom, he received an e-mail from David Myers, WorldCom controller, saying, "Do not have any more meetings with Arthur Andersen for any reason. Don't make me ask you again."[43] Brabbs was asked to record the expense adjustment on his books. He refused even when pressured from Sullivan's office to record the entry. Brabbs finally agreed to create a "management company" and record the entry there. The explanation for the entry reads, "late adjustment as instructed by Scott Sullivan."[44]

Troy Normand, a member of the accounting department, questioned the capitalization of the operating expenses. When he discussed his concerns with Sullivan, he assured Normand that "everything would be O.K."[45] According to the documents released by the House Committee, Normand "didn't communicate his concerns regarding prepaid capacity or relieving line-cost accruals to external or internal audit because he was concerned for his job and has a family to support."[46]

Investment Bankers

A Congressional committee investigating WorldCom is looking at the relationship between WorldCom and its investment bankers.[47] Salomon Smith Barney, a unit of Citigroup Inc., allocated one million shares of coveted initial public offerings to Bernard Ebbers, WorldCom's former chief executive.

The Congressional committee is particularly interested in the IPO arrangements that benefited WorldCom executives. Salomon earned millions of dollars in investment banking fees at a time when they were one of the strongest Wall Street supporters of WorldCom. Jack Grubman, the former top research analyst at Salomon, continued to issue positive reports on WorldCom, even when the financial picture was not bright. The committee is interested in whether Salomon used its "standing in the telecom IPO arena to win lucrative banking business from WorldCom by doling out shares of hot new companies to the company's top executives."[48]

Bernard Ebbers, former chief executive of WorldCom, made more than $11 million in trading profits over four years on shares of IPO offerings he received from Salomon.[49] According to the House Committee report, Ebbers often made a profit by selling within days of the initial offerings. In some cases, his share of the IPO allotment "represented a significant portion of all the shares Salomon had to give to individual investors." The committee reported: "The fact that investment banks can hand out IPO shares to individual clients who generate more underwriting business for the banks creates potential conflicts of interest across the entire investment-banking industry that we cannot simply ignore."[50]

Questions

a. Identify the ethical dilemmas that exist within the WorldCom scenario. Who benefited from the accounting fraud? Who was harmed?

b. What role did the internal auditors play in the fraud? Did they permit the company to mislead the public? Were the auditors helpful in disclosing the fraud?

c. Compare the behavior of Brabbs to that of Normand. Who, in your opinion, acted in the more ethical fashion? Describe the types of pressure directed against these men within the corporate environment of WorldCom. What might you have done, if you had been in their positions?

d. Did the investment bankers act ethically in their assignment of IPO stock to company executives who were purchasing investment services from them? Explain your answers. Even if this practice is legal, what conflict of interests may arise? Who may have been harmed?

e. Lynn Turner, former chief accountant for the SEC, said that "improper capitalization was the second most common accounting problem the SEC encountered, after improper revenue recognition."[51] Why might these two problems be so common?

Case 2.19
Contingent Liability for Toxic Waste Cleanup

Jeff Clairmont, the controller for Johnson Chemicals, has just received a notice from the Environmental Protection Agency (EPA) regarding the cleanup of the Mendota Heights Toxic Disposal Site. The cleanup is scheduled to begin in 2004 and to last for five years. Estimated costs of the cleanup are $558 million. Johnson Chemicals will be charged a share of the cleanup to represent their dumping activity over the past fifty years. Currently, this is estimated to be $48 million at a minimum, and it may go much higher. The chief financial officer, Jennifer Ordahl, has suggested ignoring the potential liability until the actual charges are received in a bill from the EPA. At most, Jennifer suggests using footnote disclosure to indicate the potential liability.

Questions

a. What is the ethical dilemma discussed in this problem?
b. Identify several alternatives available to the company, based on your knowledge of GAAP. Do GAAP rules specify the decision to be made in this situation? Is there room for interpretation in the implementation of GAAP?
c. Identify the interested parties in this decision. Who benefits? Who is harmed?
d. How would you handle the estimate of costs and potential liability? How would you convince the chief financial officer to follow your recommendation on recording this transaction?

Case 2.20
Expense Recognition

As accounting supervisor, your job is to review the daily journal entries and approve them before they are posted to the trial balance. You are watching the revenue and expense entries carefully this year, because your bonus will be based on net income. You realize that the higher the net income, the bigger your bonus will be, so you are anxious to process as many revenue transactions as possible. Your normal pattern is to process the revenue transactions the same day they are received and the expense transactions within a couple of days. Bill Anderson, the controller of the company (and your boss), has asked you to process all entries in a timely fashion at the end of the year, so the financial statements will be accurate. You wonder if you should change your policy to comply with his request, even though it will reduce your bonus.

Questions

a. Describe the accounting issue presented in this problem.
b. What is the ethical dilemma described in this scenario?
c. Identify the interested parties affected by the decision. Who benefits? Who is harmed?
d. What alternatives are available to the accounting supervisor?
e. What would you do? Explain your answer in detail.

Case 2.21
Recording Expense Entries

The controller for Anderson Electric, Ron Foss, is reviewing the year-end adjusting entries prepared by the accounting staff for approval before they are posted to the general ledger. Angela Bennett, the company president, has suggested that the December accrual for wage expense be delayed until January, because the company needs to report a higher net income for the year. The December 31 financial statements will be reviewed for a loan by the bank. The company has a better chance of getting the loan if its net income is higher, and the loan will have a lower interest rate if the company appears to be healthy. Ron is unsure whether he should comply with the president's request. It doesn't seem to Ron that it is terribly important whether the expense is recorded in December or January. Ron knows that the company needs the loan to continue paying the salaries next year, so he does not want to do anything to jeopardize his own salary.

Questions

a. What is the ethical dilemma described in this problem?
b. Based on your knowledge of generally accepted accounting principles, what is the answer to this dilemma?
c. Identify the interested parties involved in the decision. Who benefits? Who is harmed?
d. List several alternatives available to Ron.
e. What would you do? Explain your answer.

Case 2.22
Bad Debt Expense

Andrew Olson, controller for Phoenix International, has just received his new employment contract for 2003. The company has experienced rapid growth in the last year and management negotiated a bonus arrangement for its top executives. Andrew is excited about the new arrangement: if net income increases 10 percent over the prior year, he is entitled to a substantial bonus. In anticipation of the bonus, he is about to purchase a new boat on an installment plan. He has the check written for the down payment on the boat and plans to mail it today. He is confident that he can use the bad debt expense account to show that income increased by 10 percent this year. This account is just an estimate, and because he knows the increase in net income is currently above 6 percent, he should be able to manipulate this bad debt expense estimate to increase net income to the 10 percent level. If he lowers the estimate slightly, he is guaranteed his bonus and his new boat.

Questions

a. What is the accounting issue involved in this problem?
b. Should Andrew lower his estimate to permit payment of the bonus? Why?
c. Who are the interested parties in this situation? Who benefits? Who is harmed?
d. What would you do if you were in this situation? Why?
e. If Andrew does not lower his estimate, how might he explain his decision to the other executives (who might also lose their bonuses)?
f. If Andrew does lower his estimate, how can he justify his decision?

Case 2.23
Bad Debt Expense

Steve Olson and Sally Bosh, accountants at the sportswear division of Hanes Clothing, are discussing their bad debt expense allowance for 2003. Last year they based their estimate on 2 percent of net credit sales. The actual percentage written off in 2002 was 2.5 percent. Sally suggests that they increase the percentage to 4 percent for 2003. She says, "Even though I expect the bad debt write-offs to be about the same in 2003, I am a little concerned about our net income. With our current figures, our income has increased by 18 percent. That's a great increase, but probably not something we can match in 2004. If we report an increase of 18 percent in net income this year, the corporate office will expect us to achieve an 18 percent or higher growth rate in 2004. It might be simpler if we just increase our bad debt expense to 4 percent to keep our net income at a 10 percent increase. That way, we'll look good next year also, and we won't raise unreasonable expectations from the corporate office."

Questions

a. Explain why increasing the allowance for doubtful account percentage reduces net income.

b. Should Sally be concerned with the growth rate for the sportswear division when estimating the allowance for doubtful accounts? Is this improper? Explain your answer.

c. Does the estimate of bad debt expense pose an ethical dilemma for Steve and Sally? If so, state the dilemma and give your reasons.

d. Identify the interested parties involved in this decision. Who benefits? Who is harmed?

e. Does reliance on GAAP solve this dilemma? Explain your answer.

f. What alternatives are available to Sally?

g. What would you do? Why?

Case 2.24
Accounts Receivable Write-Offs

John Simpson, the controller for Marshall Steel, is reviewing the accounts receivable aging schedule for the 2003 financial statements. One of his clients, Evans Manufacturing, has recently made several management changes and completed a restructuring of its long-term debt. In the past year, *The Wall Street Journal* has carried several stories regarding its financial difficulties. At the end of 2003, Evans Manufacturing has an outstanding balance of $2,600,000 on its account, a portion of which is more than 120 days past due. Management has assured you that they will pay the balance owed as soon as they get their debt restructured. Based on this assurance, you decide not to write off the account at year-end and not to provide an allowance for a write-off in 2004. In January 2004, you notice a report in *The Wall Street Journal* that Evans Manufacturing has filed for bankruptcy. From past experience you know that in bankruptcy situations you collect less than 10 percent of the balance owed, so an adjustment probably should be made to the 2003 financial statements that have not yet been issued. Because this write-off will have a major impact on your financial statements, you want to ignore it until 2004, but you are not sure whether you can justify hiding this information from the outside reader.

Questions

a. What is the ethical dilemma described in this situation?

b. Identify the parties interested in this decision. Who benefits? Who is harmed?

c. What alternatives are available to John?

d. Would there be any temptation for John to ignore this new information about bankruptcy?

e. What would you do? Explain your decision.

Case 2.25
Year-End Shipments

24 Karet Caramels is a new candy company specializing in flavored caramels. The company has advertised widely in catalogues and has received more orders than they can ship on a daily basis. Elizabeth Hutchinson, the president, has instructed the shipping department to work overtime the last two weeks in December to ship as many orders as possible by year-end. Elizabeth says: "It is important for the company to show a profit in the first year of operations to obtain a bank loan to expand. We can recognize revenue on each sale as soon as we ship the caramels to the customers."

Questions

a. What is the accounting issue discussed in this problem? Can 24 Karet Caramels recognize revenue on the orders received or on the items shipped?
b. Is the directive given by Elizabeth unethical or is it clever business advice? Is the accounting principle of timeliness at stake here?
c. What would you do? Explain your answer.

Case 2.26
Warranty Expense

Cooperman, Inc., a pharmaceutical company, has a salary arrangement for 2004 that grants the financial vice president and several other executives $500,000 bonuses if net income increases by at least $100,000,000 in 2004. Noting that the current financial statements report an increase of $93,000,000 in net income, vice president Dick Bailey asks Elizabeth Watkins, the controller, to reduce the estimate of warranty expense by $10,000,000.

Questions

a. What is the ethical dilemma in this situation?
b. Relying on your knowledge of GAAP to answer this question, what should Elizabeth do?
c. Who is harmed if the estimate is lowered? Who benefits?
d. What would you do? Do you have a choice about what to do if your supervisor tells you to reduce the warranty expense? Consider neutrality, the possibility of bias, and who will use this information.

Case 2.27
Expense Estimates

The managers of Photoworld have a performance-based compensation plan. The performance criterion of this plan is linked to growth in earnings per share. When annual earnings per share growth is 12 percent, executives earn 110 percent of their salaries; if growth is 16 percent, executives earn 125 percent. If earnings per share increases less than 8 percent, executives receive no bonus compensation. In 2003, Bill Mattson, the controller of Photoworld, reviews the year-end estimates of warranty and bad debt expense. He calculates the increase in earnings per share to be 15 percent based on the current financial statements. Mary Christianson, his financial vice president, remarks over lunch that the estimate of bad debt expense might be decreased by a few thousand dollars, so that the increase in earnings per share would be 16.2 percent. Bill is not sure if he should alter his original estimate because of this casual comment from his boss. He thinks the original estimate was on the low side and should probably be increased rather than decreased. He does worry about his boss's suggestion because his performance evaluation is next month, and he wants to be considered a team player by her. His boss has not asked for much. Even though she will receive a large bonus, the reduction in the estimate is quite small.

Questions

a.   What is the ethical dilemma for Bill?
b.   Identify the interested parties in this situation. Who benefits if Bill increases earnings per share by decreasing the expense estimate? Who is harmed by this action?
c.   Does your knowledge of GAAP help you solve this dilemma?
d.   Should Bill's desire to increase earnings per share be a factor in his estimate of bad debt expense?
e.   How would you respond to Mary's request? How would you explain your answer to her?

EARNINGS MISSTATEMENTS

Case 2.28
Sunbeam Corporation

Sunbeam Corporation, based in Boca Raton, Louisiana, is a leading manufacturer of durable household goods and outdoor leisure products. Albert J. Dunlap, viewed by Wall Street as a turn-around genius, was hired by Sunbeam in 1996 to serve as chairman and CEO of the company. Under his direction, the company took large restructuring charges in 1996, establishing a "cookie jar" of reserves. These reserves were later reversed to meet Wall Street analysts' quarterly earnings targets. In 1997 Sunbeam executives directed the company to record excess revenue by recording sales from products that customers had not agreed to buy. Dunlap was fired in 1998, after a series of articles appeared in the press criticizing the company's accounting practices. For 1997 Sunbeam reported a restated income of $93 million, half the amount originally reported. In 1998 Sunbeam restated its financial results for most of the period when Dunlap was involved with the company.

After public disclosure of accounting irregularities under the leadership of Dunlap from 1996 to 1998, the company was subjected to an SEC investigation. In May 2001, the SEC filed a civil lawsuit against five former Sunbeam executives and Phillip E. Harlow, the Arthur Andersen partner in charge of the Sunbeam audit, accusing them of engaging in massive financial fraud.[52] The SEC suit came about two weeks after Arthur Andersen LLP agreed to pay $110 million to settle a shareholder lawsuit arising from the company's restructuring in 1996 and subsequent reporting of revenue and sales information. The lawsuit alleged that company executives painted a rosy picture of earnings growth through a series of illegal accounting actions.

Arthur Andersen says the firm believes the lawsuit filed against Harlow, is unjustified. An Andersen spokesman said, "Mr. Harlow's work for Sunbeam was performed in rigorous compliance with standards generally accepted by the profession."[53]

Questions

a.   Identify the interested parties in Sunbeam's use of "cookie jar" reserves to meet analysts' forecasts. Who benefits? Who is harmed?
b.   According to the SEC complaint, Harlow was aware of Sunbeam's improper accounting practices when he signed the audit opinion. If this is true, why might he have signed the opinion without asking Sunbeam to correct the errors? Consider the benefits and costs to the interested parties.
c.   How might Harlow defend the clean audit opinions given in 1996 and 1997 on the Sunbeam audit?

Case 2.29
Contingent Rental Fees

Allied Insurance Company, the owner of West Acres Mall, charges Software Etc. a rental fee of $25,000 per month, plus 5 percent of yearly profits over $5,000,000. Lee Grant, the owner of Software Etc., directs her accountant Roger Harrison to increase the estimate of bad debt expense, warranty costs, and depreciation on store equipment in order to keep profits at $4,900,000.

Questions

a.   What is the ethical dilemma for Roger Harrison?
b.   Who is harmed if the estimates are increased? Who benefits?
c.   Based on your knowledge of GAAP, what should Roger do?
d.   What would you do? Explain your reasons to Lee Grant.

Case 2.30
Year-End Adjusting Entries

Eduardo Garcia has just been hired as the controller for Toro Enterprises. To become familiar with the company, he is reviewing the financial statements for 2003. The previous controller completed the year-end financial statements before he left and mailed them to the holder of the long-term bonds as required by the debt covenants. Eduardo is dismayed to find several errors in the financial statements. The previous controller, George Wilson, prepared several adjusting entries on January 10, 2004. The explanations for these entries were "to avoid default on the debt covenant." George had recognized revenue on a large order received on December 28 but shipped on January 3, and had reduced depreciation expense by $2,300,000. Both of these items were designed to increase earnings per share to the required amount.

Questions

a.   What is the ethical dilemma faced by Eduardo?
b.   Based on your knowledge of GAAP, what is the appropriate accounting treatment for correcting errors?
c.   Identify interested parties affected by the errors in the financial statements presented to the bondholders. Who benefits? Who is harmed?
d.   What alternatives are available to Eduardo? Is it worse to admit to the bondholders that your predecessor made a mistake than to hide it?
e.   What would you do? Why?

Case 2.31

Performance-Based Bonuses

John Feagin and Beth Larson, accountants at Smith Manufacturing, are discussing the year-end adjusting process. Beth has just had lunch with the president of the company, Lindsay Norton, and Lindsay suggested that Beth could be a good friend by doing her part to increase net income for the current year. Lindsay has just purchased a new house, and she is relying on her bonus payment to furnish the home. If Beth could make sure that net income increased by at least 10 percent this year, Lindsay would receive a substantial bonus. Lindsay suggested that Beth should aggressively accrue revenues at year-end and delay recording as many expenses as possible. Beth is confused by this request and asks John for advice.

Questions

a.   Explain why Lindsay's request would increase net income.
b.   What is the ethical dilemma faced by Beth in this situation?
c.   Identify the parties affected by the decision to increase net income. Who benefits? Who is harmed?
d.   What alternatives are available to Beth? What advice should John offer?
e.   What does Beth stand to gain by complying with Lindsay's request? What does she stand to lose?
f.   What advice would you give Beth? How would you explain your position to John?

Case 2.32
Operating Loans

John Haug, controller of Tenant Company, is reviewing the year-end financial statements with Tom Henry, the company president. The financial statements currently report a net income of $10,563,480 before adjusting entries. Tom is applying for a bank loan to build a new manufacturing facility and would like to report a net income of at least $12,750,000. Tom suggests accruing several sales based on orders received, even though the goods will not be shipped at year-end. He says, "If we record sales revenue for these two large orders, our net income should be more than $12,750,000. We will never notice the loss of these sales next year, because when we build the new manufacturing facility our sales revenue will dramatically increase."

Questions

a.   What is the ethical dilemma described in this case?
b.   Based on your knowledge of GAAP, can you resolve this dilemma?
c.   What alternatives are available to John?

d. What would you do? Would your answer change if you knew the financial statements would not be audited, so it would be unlikely that your "error" would be caught?

e. Would your answer change if you knew that Tom's bonus depended on increasing net income to $12,750,000? Why?

f. Would you change your mind if you knew the president would fire you if you did not increase net income to his goal of $12,750,000? Is your answer ethical?

Case 2.33
Shipping Terms

Woodlawn Exports sells household goods to companies in several foreign countries. Most items take two to three weeks to arrive at their destination. Goods are usually shipped FOB destination. John Andrews, the chief financial officer of Woodlawn, has asked Elizabeth Sanders, a controller, to alter the invoices for the last two weeks of the year, to read "FOB shipping point" rather then "FOB destination." John says, "Earnings for the current year will look much better if we include several major sales made in the last half of December. Besides, after we deliver the goods to the shipper, haven't we done everything needed to recognize revenue? I think this change will allow us to pay bonuses to management."

Questions

a. What is the accounting issue discussed in this problem? Why does altering the shipping terms alter revenue recognition?

b. What is the ethical dilemma described in this problem?

c. Identify the parties who are harmed if Elizabeth complies with John's request. Which parties benefit?

d. Does Elizabeth have a choice if her supervisor has asked her to alter the invoices?

e. What would you do?

Case 2.34
Estimating a Future Expense

The cost associated with mothballing a nuclear power plant at the end of its useful life, approximately 20 years in the future, will be paid by the utility company when the plant is obsolete at the end of the 20-year period. When should the expense be recognized for this expenditure? Current utility users receive the benefit of this plant. Do accounting rules require them to pay the cost in terms of increased utility rates by including the expense of the future mothballing in their rates, or should the expense be delayed for 20 years, until the cash is actually paid out?

Questions

a. To record an expense, the accountant must be able to estimate the amount of the expenditure. Will it be difficult to estimate an expense to be paid 20 years in the future?

b. Should the expense of mothballing the power plant be recorded over the estimated useful life of the power plant (20 years) or be delayed until the cash is paid out at the end of the 20 years? Despite the difficulty of estimating the expense, based on your knowledge of GAAP, how would you answer this question? Consider both the matching principle and the concept of conservatism in your response.

c. What is the ethical dilemma described in this question?

d. Identify the parties affected by this decision. Who benefits? Who is harmed?

e. What decision would you make? Justify your decision.

Endnotes

1 Sharon Young, "Qwest says it plans to restate financial results for 2000, 2001," *The Wall Street Journal*, July 29, 2002.

2 Key facts for Qwest Communications International, http: //www.wsj.com, September 17, 2002.

3 Dennis Berman, "Regulators are taking a look at Andersen's "swaps' method," *The Wall Street Journal*, March 19, 2002.

4 Susan Pulliam and Rebecca Blumenstein, "SEC broadens investigation into revenue-boosting tricks—Agency finds new focus as 'round trip' deals appear to be widespread," *The Wall Street Journal*, May 15, 2002.

5 Henry Sender, "SEC deals blow to telecom by rejecting capacity swaps," *The Wall Street Journal*, August 21, 2002.

6 Deborah Solomon and Susan Pulliam, "SEC adopts tougher position on Qwest accounting methods," *The Wall Street Journal*, June 26, 2002.

7 Deborah Solomon, "Qwest cuts full-year outlook, nears risky debt-ebitda ratio," *The Wall Street Journal*, August 9, 2002.

8 Gardiner Harris, "SEC is probing Bristol-Myers over sales-incentive accounting," *The Wall Street Journal*, July 12, 2002.

9 Gardiner Harris, "Bristol-Myers says may restate results in wholesale overbuys," *The Wall Street Journal*, August 8, 2002.

10 Jerry Guidera, "Computer Associates' revenue is probed by federal officials," *The Wall Street Journal*, May 20, 2002.

11 "Annual Earnings for Computer Associates," *The Wall Street Journal*, September 18, 2002.

12 Jerry Guidera, "Computer Associates probe widens; former auditors are subpoenaed," *The Wall Street Journal*, May 16, 2002.

13 Jerry Guidera, "Computer Associates' revenue is probed by federal officials," *The Wall Street Journal*, May 20, 2002.

14 Marcelo Prine, "Computer Associates shareholders approve 11 nominees for board," *The Wall Street Journal*, August 28, 2002.

15 Key facts for AOL Time Warner, Inc., http: //www.wsj.com, September 18, 2002.

16 Alec Klein, "Unconventional transactions boosted sales; amid big merger, company resisted dot-com. collapse," *The Washington Post*, July 18, 2002; Jonathan Weil, "AOL could soon need to take another gargantuan write-off," *The Wall Street Journal*, August 23, 2002.

17 Jonathan Weil, "AOL could soon need to take another gargantuan write-off," *The Wall Street Journal*, August 23, 2002.

18 James Bandler and Mark Maremont, "How ex-accountant added up to trouble for humbled Xerox," *The Wall Street Journal*, June 28, 2001.

19 James Bandler, "Xerox faces criminal inquiry tied to financial restatement," *The Wall Street Journal*, September 24, 2002.

20 Key facts for Xerox, Inc. http: //www.wsj.com, September 18, 2002.

21 U.S. Securities and Exchange Commission, "Xerox settles SEC enforcement action charging company with fraud," http://www.sec.gov/news.

22 James Bandler and Mark Maremont, "How ex-accountant added up to trouble for humbled Xerox," *The Wall Street Journal*, June 28, 2001.

23 Dennis Berman and Susan Pulliam, "Global Crossing's initial bid to settle SEC case is rejected," *The Wall Street Journal*, August 28, 2002.

24 Dennis Berman, "SEC probes Global Crossing's swaps in interviews with firm's salespeople," *The Wall Street Journal*, May 10, 2002.

25 Ibid.

26 Dennis Berman, "Three telecom companies testify they cut side deals with Qwest," *The Wall Street Journal*, September 25, 2002.

27 Ibid.

28 Ibid.

[29] "Global Crossing workers knew of swap trouble, e-mails show," *The Wall Street Journal*, September 20, 2002.

[30] Barbara Martinez, "Merck books co-payments to pharmacies as revenue," *The Wall Street Journal*, June 21, 2002; Barbara Martinez, "Merck recorded $12.4 billion in revenue it never collected," *The Wall Street Journal*, July 8, 2002.

[31] Kathryn Kranhold, "SEC seeks information on Mirant's accounting," *The Wall Street Journal*, August 6, 2002.

[32] Ibid.

[33] Steve Stecklow, "Colleges inflate SATs and graduation rates in popular guidebooks," *The Wall Street Journal*, April 5, 1995.

[34] Nina Munk, "Now you see it, now you don't," *Forbes*, June 5, 1995.

[35] Key Facts for WorldCom, Inc., http: //www.wsj.com, September 25, 2002.

[36] Jared Sandberg, Rebecca Blumenstein, and Shawn Young, "WorldCom internal probe uncovers massive fraud, " *The Wall Street Journal,* June 26, 2002.

[37] "SEC statement concerning World Come," http://www.sec.gov/news/press/2002-9.4.htm, June 26, 2002.

[38] Jared Sandberg and Susan Pulliam, "WorldCom finds more errors; restatement will be $7.2 billion," *The Wall Street Journal,* August 9, 2002.

[39] Susan Pulliam and Jared Sandberg, "New WorldCom report to SEC will acknowledge more flaws," *The Wall Street Journal,* 2002.

[40] Deborah Solomon and Susan Pulliam, "U.S., pushing WorldCom case, indicts ex-CFO and his aide," *The Wall Street Journal,* August 29, 2002.

[41] Deborah Solomon, "WorldCom's ex-controller pleads guilty to 3 counts," *The Wall Street Journal,* September 27, 2002.

[42] Yochi J. Dreazen and Deborah Solomon, "Andersen ignored warnings on WorldCom, memos show," *The Wall Street Journal,* July 15, 2002

[43] Yochi J. Drwazen, "WorldCom's Myers attempted to stifle accounting questions," *The Wall Street Journal,* August 27, 2002.

[44] Yochi J. Dreazen and Deborah Solomon, "Andersen ignored warnings on WorldCom, memos show," *The Wall Street Journal,* July 15, 2002

[45] Ibid.

[46] Ibid.

[47] Charles Gasparino, Tom Hamburger, and Deborah Solomon, "Salomon made IPO allocations available to its favored clients," *The Wall Street Journal,* August 28, 2002.

[48] Charles Gasparino, "Salomon admits that it sent hot IPOs WorldCom's way," *The Wall Street Journal,* August 27, 2002.

[49] Suzanne Craig, "Ebbers made over $11 million on IPO shares from Salomon," *The Wall Street Journal,* September 3, 2002.

[50] Ibid.

[51] James S. Granelli, James F. Peltz, and Thomas J. Mulligan, "The WorldCom scandal: what went wrong? SEC targets top execs; errors shock analysts," *The Los Angeles Times,* July 27, 2002.

[52] Jonathan Weil, "5 Sunbean Ex-Executives Sued by SEC," *The Wall Street Journal*, May 16, 2001.

[53] Ibid.

Chapter 3
The Balance Sheet

Accountants must be alert to companies' efforts to improve the appearance of the balance sheet, either by overstating assets or by understating liabilities. For example, companies overstate assets by failing to write off uncollectible accounts receivable and by leaving obsolete inventory on their books. Companies may also change the depreciation lives of their assets to decrease depreciation expense. Companies may understate liabilities by failing to record expenses incurred at year-end or by recording debt in affiliated companies to keep the debt off the balance sheet. Misclassification of assets and liabilities between current and long-term accounts is sometimes used by management to avoid violating ratio or cash stipulations of loan agreements.

Problems related to the balance sheet are presented in two categories in the chapter: (1) assets and (2) liabilities and owners equity.

ASSETS

Case 3.1
Surprise Cash Counts

Helen Flynn, the auditor for Roberts Garden Supply, is making surprise cash counts of the petty cash funds at the store's four locations. She arrives at the Fifth Street store at lunchtime and is advised that Kathy, the custodian of the petty cash funds, will not be available until later. Kathy is currently on the phone and then has plans for lunch. Kathy makes an appointment, asking Helen to return at 2 PM. When Helen returns, the cash box contains several receipts, including some that are handwritten. Each receipt has today's date, and Helen notices that the cash consists of only new $10 bills. The receipts and the cash total the normal balance of $100.

Questions

a. What is the accounting issue discussed in this problem? Based on your knowledge of GAAP, what should Helen do?
b. What ethical dilemma faces Helen?
c. Discuss two or three internal control features that might have prevented this problem. What internal control feature did Helen violate?
d. What would you do? Explain your answer.

Case 3.2
Cash from Operations on the Statement of Cash Flows

A debt covenant for the bonds issued by St. Andrews Hospital requires the company to report cash from operations of $1,000,000 at the end of each year of operations. The controller, Steve Savage, reviews the cash flow statement on December 1, 2003 to determine if the hospital will meet this covenant by December 31, 2003. Currently the cash flow statement shows a balance of $900,000 for the net cash provided by operations. Steve's supervisor, Julie Peterson, believes that he can increase this balance by year-end either by decreasing the accounts receivable balance or by increasing the accounts payable balance. Steve knows that it is impossible to decrease the accounts receivable balance by year-end. Most of the revenue comes from third-party insurance payments, and there is no way to convince the insurance companies to pay faster. The only way to increase the accounts payable balance by the necessary amount is to delay payment of the weekly bills for the last three weeks in December. This action will make creditors unhappy, but it is the easiest way to meet the debt covenant requirement.

Questions

a. Will taking Julie's suggestion have the desired result? Explain the accounting impact.
b. Does Steve face an ethical dilemma with Julie's suggestions for altering the statement of cash flows? If so, describe this dilemma.
c. Identify the interested parties affected by the decision to increase the accounts payable balance at year-end. Who benefits from this decision? Who is harmed?
d. Suggest other alternatives that might be available to Steve.
e. What would you do? Explain your answer.

Case 3.3
Classifying Notes Receivable

The balance sheet for Home Interiors contains several 6- and 24-month notes receivable. The 6-month notes are included in the current asset portion of the balance sheet; the 24-month notes are listed as noncurrent assets. Payment on the 24-month notes is expected to occur in a timely fashion at the end of the two year period. Payment on the 6-month notes, which was scheduled to occur four months after year-end, will be delayed by one year. The customer holding the notes has contacted Home Interiors and has been granted a one year extension. Sue Garness, controller for Home Interiors, is reviewing the 2003 financial statements. She suggests reclassifying the 6-month notes as noncurrent assets, because collection will be delayed beyond one year. Her supervisor, Jim Christianson, prefers listing the notes as current assets. Jim is concerned about the current ratio of Home Interiors. If the notes are classified as noncurrent assets, the current ratio will decline and the company may fail to receive the bank loan needed for operations in 2004.

Questions

a. What is the accounting issue involved in the reclassification of the notes receivable? What do GAAP rules suggest in this situation?
b. What does Sue's supervisor gain by not following GAAP rules?
c. Identify the interested parties involved in this situation. Who benefits? Who is harmed?
d. Considering the possible harm to the parties, what is the ethical dilemma for Sue Garness?
e. Should Sue reclassify the notes? Explain your reason.
f. How should Sue explain her decision to her boss?

Case 3.4
Inventory Purchases

Jean Pitman, the manager of the purchasing department for United Stores, has just returned from a staff meeting. The controller, Ernie Larson, has asked Jean to purchase a large number of circuit boards at year-end as a means of lowering net income for United Stores. Jean is not an accountant and does not understand much about net income, but she is confused by this request. Her job, as manager of the purchasing department, is to buy circuit boards (the major inventory item for United Stores) at the best possible price. At the beginning of the year, she was purchasing the boards for $12 per board. The price is currently $20 per board. Normally she would wait until next year to see if the price drops, but she is now forced to purchase boards at $20 each to meet the request of the controller. The company uses the LIFO method of inventory valuation, but she doesn't know what this means. She wonders if it is "right" to use the purchase of an inventory item to manipulate net income and has asked you for advice, since she knows you are taking an accounting class.

Questions

a. Why has the controller suggested this year-end inventory purchase to lower net income? How will this purchase lower net income?
b. What is the ethical dilemma, if any, in this situation?
c. Identify the interested parties in the decision. Who benefits? Who is harmed?
d. Is this a good business decision or is it an unethical decision on the part of the controller?
e. What would you do? Explain your answer.
f. If United Stores had been using the FIFO method of inventory valuation, would the controller have suggested the year-end purchase? Why?
g. If inventory prices were falling, rather than rising, would the controller have suggested this purchase? Why?

Case 3.5
Inventory Purchases

John Jacobson, purchasing manager for Johnson Controls, has just received an offer to make an inventory purchase at a special discount. The offer runs from December 10th to January 10th. John is tempted to make the purchase in the current year, because he is evaluated on his ability to purchase inventory items at competitive prices. This purchase would make him look good and would assure that he receives a raise this year. He asks Fran Dexter, the controller, to approve this purchase. Fran says: "Well, since we use the LIFO method of inventory, this would have a major impact on net income. I'm not sure if it would be right for me to approve this inventory purchase."

Questions

a. Describe the accounting issue posed in this problem. Why is the controller concerned about the year-end inventory purchase?
b. What is the ethical dilemma described in this situation? Is it right to make a large inventory purchase at the end of the year that will make the purchasing manager look good, even though it would decrease net income?
c. Identify the interested parties affected by this decision. Who benefits? Who is harmed?
d. What would you do? Explain your answer.

Case 3.6
LIFO Inventory Liquidation

Toys for Kids uses the LIFO method of inventory valuation. In January 2004, Naomi Alexson reviews the 2003 financial statements. She notices that the company had a LIFO inventory liquidation in 2003 because the ending inventory was lower than the beginning inventory. Jamie Nelson, the company president, tells Naomi that an inventory liquidation is unacceptable. The president is concerned about the income taxes that will have to be paid. She encourages Naomi to record several orders for inventory items ordered on December 30, 2003, and received on January 5, 2003, in the 2003 inventory amount. Jamie suggests that Naomi call the vendors and ask them to date the bills on December 31, 2003, so the company has documentation for the inventory purchase in 2003.

Questions

a. What is the ethical dilemma described in this problem?
b. Identify the interested parties involved in this decision. Who benefits? Who is harmed?
c. List several alternatives available to Naomi.
d. What would you do? Explain your answer.

e. If Naomi had known about the inventory liquidation in December 2003 and had ordered and received the inventory items in December, would you change your previous answer? Explain in detail.

f. Why is planning ahead ethical in these circumstances, but why might fixing a problem after the year-end not be ethical?

Case 3.7
Allocating Costs for a Basket Purchase of Assets

Anderson Office Systems has just purchased a new manufacturing plant in San Jose, California. Jose Mendez and Romar Rodriguez, accountants at Anderson, are discussing the allocation of the $500 million purchase price between land, building, and equipment. Jim suggests allocating as much of the purchase price as possible to the building and equipment, since they are depreciable. Sharon isn't sure if this allocation method makes sense, since the value of the land in California represents a sizable portion of the purchase price.

Questions

a. Discuss the accounting issue in this problem. Do GAAP rules tell you how to determine the value of the land and the building in a joint purchase? In other words, can you answer this question by reliance on GAAP rules? Explain your answer.

b. What is the ethical dilemma in this situation?

c. Identify the interested parties involved in this decision. Who benefits? Who is harmed?

d. What would you do? Does your decision faithfully represent the economic situation? How would you explain your decision to Maria Smith, your supervisor?

Case 3.8
Recording Modifications to Office Equipment

Robert Sherman and Terry Bell, accountants for Chatworth Advertising, are reviewing the current year's expenditures in the repair and maintenance account. Bell questions whether the installation of new disk drives on one hundred office computers should be expensed when the drives improve the operating efficiency of the computers. She argues that the installation should be capitalized because it increases the future service potential of the computers. Sherman disagrees.

Questions

a. What is the ethical dilemma in this situation? Are Bell and Sherman each acting unethically?

b. Assume you agree with Bell. Discuss the argument that Bell might make to convince Sherman that capitalizing the disk drives is the proper accounting treatment.

c. Assume you agree with Sherman. What argument might Sherman use to convince Bell that the disk drives should be expensed?

d. What would you do? Which of these arguments do you believe is the most compelling, from an accounting point of view?

e. Identify at least one argument that is incorrect in convincing the other accountant to select your method.

Case 3.9
Alternative Sources of Cash

Sandra Madson, the founder and the owner of a major portion of the stock for Computer Technology, wants to raise cash by issuing bonds to open four new offices. Emily Christenson, who owns 35 percent of the stock but doesn't work in the company, wants to raise money by issuing stock. In this way, Emily can purchase all the shares of the stock and take control of the company. Sandra cannot compete to purchase the new stock because she does not have the funds. Emily has plans to expand the company by opening offices in several cities and would like to make Sandra a minority owner.

Questions

a. What is the ethical dilemma described in this problem?

b. If the company can't afford to take on the debt, is Sandra acting ethically by issuing debt?

c. Is Emily acting ethically by trying to take over Sandra's company?

d. Identify the parties affected by each method of raising cash. In each case, who benefits? Who is harmed?

e. Does Sandra have other alternatives?

f. What would you do? Explain your answer.

See C 3.4

Case 3.10
Investment Securities

Matt Adams, the controller of Plunkett's Furniture Store, and Becky Williams, the staff accountant, prepare the year-end financial statements. Matt wants to transfer some of the trading securities in the investment account to the available-for-sale account, because he does not want to reduce net income by the decline in fair value of these securities. Becky asks Matt whether they intend to hold the securities for longer than one month and Matt replies, "Whatever it takes to get these securities out of the trading account. Even if we have to borrow money instead of selling the securities, it would be worth it to avoid reporting the decline in value on the income statement."

Questions

a. What is the accounting issue discussed in this problem? Why does Matt want to transfer the securities from the trading to the available-for-sale account? Why does Becky ask Matt if the securities will be held for more than one month?
b. Based on your knowledge of GAAP, how would you resolve this dilemma?
c. What is the ethical dilemma facing Becky in this problem?
d. Identify the parties affected by the decision to reclassify trading securities as available-for-sale securities. Who benefits by this decision? Who is harmed?
e. Would Matt be making the same recommendation if the securities had increased in value?
f. Assume Becky's supervisor tells her to make this change. Does she have a choice? As an accountant, is it her responsibility to make sure that the decision is a reasonable one, or is it her job to "do what she's told"?
g. What would you do? Explain your decision.

Case 3.11
Selling Investment Securities

Jose Garcia and Sergio Mendes review the year-end financial statements. Jose is concerned about net income because the owners of the company had hoped for a 15 percent increase from 2003 to 2004 and the numbers support only a 9 percent increase. Jose is afraid that the raises and bonuses for management will not be high enough unless he thinks of a way to increase net income. Sergio suggests selling the available-for-sale securities that have increased in value and holding until next year the securities that have decreased in value. Jose is unsure whether this approach of selectively selling securities is ethical.

Questions

a. Explain the accounting issue involved in this problem. Why did Sergio suggest selling only the securities that have increased in value? How will this solve their problem? Might Sergio have made the same suggestion for the trading securities?
b. Is there an ethical dilemma described in this problem? If so, what is it?
c. Identify the parties affected by the decision to sell the securities that have increased in value. Who benefits from this decision? Who is harmed?
d. What would you do? Why? Is a concern for management bonuses appropriate for an accountant?

Case 3.12
Sale of Investment Securities

Sam Clauson, president of Computer Software, exclaims, "Net income is too high! I never thought I'd say that. But if we grow 20 percent this year, the parent company will expect us to grow 22 percent next year. There is no way we can sustain that kind of growth. Everything just fell into place this year, but with the economy worsening, there is no way we can duplicate this year's sales. We must reduce our net income to a more manageable growth rate this year, or we'll never meet our targets next year and the company will not give us a raise. Do you have any ideas about how to lower net income?" Jennifer Korsmo, the controller of the company, replies, "We have several large available-for-sale securities that have decreased in value over the year. It would be a good time to sell the securities, realize the loss, and lower our net income in the process. We can always use the cash from the securities sales to purchase additional securities. The market is at a low, and it is a good time to buy securities at rock-bottom prices. This is the best way to lower net income."

Questions

a.   What is the accounting issue discussed in this problem? Will the security sale have the desired affect on net income? Might Jennifer also recommend this sale for the trading securities?
b.   Is there an ethical dilemma described in the problem of the selective selling of the securities? If so, what is it?
c.   Identify the parties affected by this decision. Who benefits? Who is harmed?
d.   What would you do? Why?

Case 3.13
Subsidiary Ledger Reconciliation

Sharon Erickson is preparing the aging report for the outstanding accounts receivable at the end of the third quarter. The aging report is needed by management to review accounts that are uncollectible so the balances can be written off. The balance in the accounts receivable subsidiary ledger is $2,219,000 greater than the accounts receivable balance in the general ledger. Sharon has no idea how to reconcile the subsidiary account to the general ledger in the short time remaining before the management meeting. She decides to provide them with the incorrect numbers, hoping that they will not compare the subsidiary total to the general ledger.

Questions

a.   Identify the accounting issue in this problem.
b.   What is the ethical dilemma described in this problem?
c.   Identify the parties affected by this decision. Who benefits? Who is harmed?

d.   What would you do? Explain your answer. Does your decision represent the economic situation?

Case 3.14
Cash Discounts

Jon Evert, controller for Arnold Manufacturing, has hired Martha Anderson to work in the accounts payable area. Martha will be responsible for paying bills promptly to take advantage of all cash discounts. The previous accounts payable accountant, Sara Esteban, is responsible for training Martha to do her new job. Sara says that she has been following the policy of writing all checks on the last day of the discount period (10 days after the invoice date) and then holding the checks for five days before mailing them. According to Sara, her supervisors have been very pleased with her performance in this area and have given her bonuses based on her commitment to the company. Sara suggests that Martha continue this policy of paying bills. "Customers don't complain because they are happy to be paid. If they do question the amount of our payment, we can always blame it on the computer or the mailroom."

Questions

a.   What is the ethical dilemma described in this case?
b.   Identify the interested parties in this situation. Who benefits? Who is harmed?
c.   Based on your knowledge of GAAP, what should Martha do? Will her supervisors be more or less happy with her if she mails the check on time?
d.   What would you do? Explain your answer.

Case 3.15
Recording Unauthorized Cash Discounts

Red Baron Airlines purchases supplies, fuel, and food services from a variety of vendors. The financial vice president has just instructed Jim Stuart, the accounts payable accounting supervisor, to pay all invoices on the 25th day, but to take all discounts offered. He said, "If the vendor complains, we can always find another supplier. We purchase such a large quantity of goods that most suppliers will let us do anything, just to keep our business. I hope we don't have to follow this practice very long, but it should help our cash flow situation at the present."

Questions

a.   What is the ethical dilemma described in this situation?
b.   Identify the interested parties harmed by the financial vice president's decision. Are there any parties that benefit from this situation?

c.   From a business point of view, is this a good practice to follow? What are the potential consequences of this practice?

d.   From an ethical point of view, is this a good practice to follow?

e.   What would you do? Explain your decision.

Case 3.16
Cash Shortages

Wendy Norland has just started working for a major department store as a sales associate. Jennifer is training her in the duties of the new position. At the end of the first day, Wendy and Jennifer are counting the cash in their drawer and reconciling cash receipts to the cash register total. Jennifer says: "We use a cash envelope to deal with cash differences. If you are short tonight, take the cash out of this envelope to balance out. The nights when you have extra cash, place the extra cash in the envelope and report that you were even. This method allows you to "look good" because your cash balances out. It is easier than reporting an "error" every day when your cash is over or short. I'm so glad you will be working with us. It looks like you will catch on to the way we do business here quickly."

Questions

a.   What is the ethical dilemma described in this problem?

b.   Based on your knowledge of GAAP, what should you do? Why might it be difficult to follow GAAP in this situation?

c.   From the perspective of internal control, what are some of the problems in using a cash over-and-short envelope?

d.   What would you do? Explain your answer.

Case 3.17
Changing Asset Lives

Luke Jacobson and Erin Jablonski are reviewing the financial statements for Jones Manufacturing for 2004. Sales have declined in the last year due to the economy and the unfavorable exchange rates with their foreign customers. The financial vice president, Luke Jacobson, suggests lengthening asset lives to reduce depreciation expense. Machinery purchased for $1,800,000 in 2001 was originally estimated to have a life of 9 years with a salvage value of $50,000 at the end of the period. Depreciation has been recorded for three years on this basis. Jacobson wants to change the estimated life of the machinery to 12 years with a salvage value of $100,000. Accountant Erin Jablonski disagrees with Jacobson. She says it would be unethical to increase net income in this manner.

Questions

a.   Is the change in asset lives unethical, or simply a good business decision by an astute vice president? Explain your answer.
b.   Who are the interested parties affected by this decision? Who benefits? Who is harmed?
c.   What would you do?

Case 3.18
Cash Salary Payments

Joe's Taco Shop employs 50 people in its restaurant. Forty employees are full-time and the rest are part-time. He pays the salary expense of the part-time employees in cash. No deductions are made from the checks to cover social security tax or federal income tax. The employees are simply paid their hourly wage. By paying these employees in cash, Joe avoids matching their social security deductions and paying federal and state unemployment tax and workers' compensation on the employees. Joe believes that the employees prefer to be paid in cash because then they can choose whether to report this income on their income tax returns. Joe has hired an accountant to prepare the monthly financial statement.

Questions

a.   Is Joe's method of payment legal?
b.   What is the ethical dilemma for the accountant hired by the restaurant? Do you believe the accountant is aware of the cash payments to the employees?
c.   Identify the parties affected by the decision to make cash payments to the part-time employees. Who benefits? Who is harmed?
d.   What would you do?

LIABILITIES AND OWNERS EQUITY

Case 3.19
Classifying Liabilities as Short-Term or Long-Term

ABC Construction Company has a $100 million long-term note payable. The loan covenants relating to this note require the company to maintain a current ratio of 2:1. Paul Anderson, the controller for the company, is preparing the financial disclosure report for the insurance company that holds the note. This report for the last year is due by March 15. He notices that the current ratio has dropped below 2:1, based on a short-term loan negotiated with the bank for operating expenses. Paul is concerned about the $100 million note being due immediately if the company violates the loan covenant. The company would not have the money to pay off the $100 million note. This might be a serious problem for the company unless they can improve the current ratio. The treasurer of the company has suggested that they reclassify the note they just took out as long-term rather than current, even though it has a payment date of nine months. He also suggested paying off a portion of the short-term liabilities with cash to reduce the amount of the current liabilities.

Questions

a.   Discuss whether the two possibilities suggested by the treasurer would have the desired outcome.
b.   What is the ethical dilemma described in this problem?
c.   Identify the interested parties affected by the decision to increase the current ratio to the desired level. Who benefits? Who is harmed?
d.   Identify several alternatives available to Paul. What actions most faithfully represent the economic situation of the company?
e.   What would you do? Explain your answer.
f.   Would it make a difference if the treasurer suggested that sometimes people are required to be team players in this company? Or that team players are rewarded?
g.   Would your decision be different if this was your first job and if you had many school loans to repay and it would be difficult to get another job?

Case 3.20
Bond Sinking Funds

Dakota Hospital has established a bond sinking fund as required by its debt agreement for the bonds payable. The current balance in the sinking fund is $13 million. Dakota Hospital needs to borrow $3 million to cover its operating debts for 60 days when a third-party insurance payment for Medicare and Medicaid is delayed due to a shut-down in the federal government. Steve Carlson, the trustee of the sinking fund, is unsure about allowing this transfer. He is confident that the hospital will be able to repay the loan, with interest, in 90 days, but this is not an authorized payment from the sinking fund.

The auditor will conduct the yearly audit next month, and he is not sure what he would tell the auditor about the transfer.

Questions

a. What is the ethical dilemma discussed in this situation?
b. Identify several alternatives available to the hospital.
c. Which interested parties would be harmed by the unauthorized transfer of funds? Which parties would benefit?
d. What would you do? Why?

Case 3.21
Classifying Liabilities

Jefferson Manufacturing has a long-term note payable on its books that requires the company to maintain a current ratio of 2:1. If the company defaults on any of the debt covenants, the note is immediately payable. At December 20, the current ratio is 1.8:1. Jessica Beardsley, the controller, considers several actions to increase the current ratio by December 31. Perhaps the easiest thing, she thinks, would be to transfer a $500,000 note payable (due in 10 months) to a long-term liability account. This note has a provision allowing the company to extend the loan by 12 months if the lender believes it is a good credit risk. Management had not planned to request an extension of the loan, but it would be simple enough to tell the auditors it had planned to request this extension, so the note should have a 22-month due date. With this transfer, the current ratio will be 2.2:1, within the bounds of the debt covenant.

Questions

a. What is the ethical dilemma described in this problem?
b. Based on your knowledge of GAAP, what is the correct decision?
c. Why might the accountant be tempted to disregard the GAAP rules?
d. Identify the interested parties affected by this decision. Who benefits? Who is harmed?
e. What alternatives are available to Jessica?
f. What would you do? Why?

Case 3.22
Purchase of Treasury Stock

Johnson Controls has several debt covenants related to its bonds payable. One covenant requires Johnson Controls to keep earnings per share above $5.00. A month before year-end, Harvey Johnson, the controller, is working on the 2003 annual report. Based on estimated earnings and the weighted average number of shares of stock outstanding, the earnings per share is currently $4.25. The only way the company can increase earnings per share to reach $5.00 in one month is to borrow money and purchase treasury stock. If the company borrows money for this purpose, however, it will find it difficult to negotiate an operating loan during the first quarter of the next year. Harvey isn't sure about purchasing the treasury stock because, although it will solve the problem of the debt covenant this month, it will create a cash flow problem in the following year.

Questions

a.   Does the purchase of treasury stock have the required outcome on earnings per share?
b.   What is the ethical dilemma described in this problem?
c.   If the company violates the debt covenant, what might the creditors do?
d.   Identify several alternatives available to Harvey.
e.   What interested parties benefit by Harvey's decision to purchase treasury stock? What parties are harmed?
f.   What would you do in this situation? Would your answer change if Johnson Controls had excess cash, and purchasing treasury stock was one of several alternatives for spending the cash?
g.   Would your answer change if the current price of the stock was unusually high? Why? If the current price of the stock was at a five-year low? Explain.

Case 3.23
Deferred Tax Liability

Sandra Schield, the financial vice president of Atlas Steel Company, and Keith Miller, the controller, are reviewing the tax accrual for 2003. The net deferred tax liability is $2,000,000. Of this amount, $500,000 will be paid within one year; the balance will be paid over the next ten years. Sandra wants to classify the entire balance as a long-term liability, but Keith argues that $500,000 of the balance is most properly a short-term liability because it will be paid within one year. Sandra responds by saying, "We have never classified deferred tax liabilities as short-term. Doing so will reduce the company's current ratio. This will endanger our prospects for getting a major loan from the bank."

Questions

a.   Explain how classifying a portion of the deferred tax liability as short-term affects the current ratio.
b.   Is there an ethical dilemma in this situation?
c.   Who is harmed by classifying the liability as long-term?
d.   Based on your knowledge of GAAP, what is the answer to this problem?
e.   What would you do? Explain your answer.

Case 3.24
Discounts on Accounts Payable

Simmons College recently hired Bob Miller as its controller. Bob has several years of experience working for a major manufacturing company. He has been hired to prepare the monthly financial statements and to closely monitor the cash flow situation at the college. Jason West, the current accounts payable accountant, is excited about the new ideas that Bob will bring to the college for managing cash flows. Jason and Bob are reviewing the accounts payable report for the prior month. Bob says, "Well, I can see one change that will be very easy to make and will allow us to have greater control over our cash payments. Most companies in the business world take discounts when they pay their bills, even if the discount period has expired. I thought everyone did this. Most customers don't complain, and if they do, we can always pay them the difference next month. It's a good thing Simmons College hired someone from business to tell them how things are really done." Jason is not sure whether he should follow Bob's advice on paying the bills late and taking discounts after the discount period. Simmons College has always worked hard to maintain a good relationship within the business community. Jason is afraid that if he begins the practice of delaying payments, yet taking discounts, the reputation of the college will be damaged. However, Jason is anxious to follow the practice of the business community, and perhaps he does not realize how things are done in the business world.

Questions

a. Do you believe that Bob's assessment of the way things are done in the business community is accurate? If Bob is correct, does this mean that the college as a business should do things the way everyone else does?
b. What is the ethical dilemma described in this problem?
c. Will the relationship between Simmons College and the business community be harmed by this practice or will others recognize that the college is just joining "the real business world"? Will the college be harmed if it treats its creditors in this way?
d. What alternatives are available to Jason?
e. Which parties are harmed by Bob's suggestion? Which parties benefit?
f. What would you do? Write a brief paragraph explaining your decision to Bob.

Case 3.25
Debt Covenants

Tom Anderson, the controller for Plains Software, is reviewing the financial statements for the previous month. He is preparing the report to the insurance company that holds the bonds payable issued to finance the plant expansion. This report must be completed by the fifth of each month. Tom is horrified to find that the cash balance dropped below $300,000 the previous month, so technically the company is in default on its loan. This violation is serious, because now the $10,000,000 in long-term debt becomes a short-term liability that bondholders might decide to collect immediately. Tom suggests that Jason, the accountant in charge of cash receipts, hold the books open until November 1 to include these cash receipts in the October 31 cash balance. This extra day's receipts would increase the cash balance to the desired $300,000 mark.

Questions

a. What is the ethical dilemma described in this problem? Is Tom's suggestion only a minor matter? Is the suggestion inappropriate, from an accounting perspective?
b. Identify the interested parties involved in this decision. Who benefits by keeping the books open? Who is harmed?
c. In addition to complying or not complying with Tom's request, might Jason telephone an insurance representative? What might Jason say?
d. Would you comply with Tom's request? Explain your decision.

Case 3.26
Classifying Notes Payable

Chris Sanderson and Jeremy Uttke prepare the statement of cash flows for the Oak Grove Management Company. It is their responsibility to determine the cash flow from operations to calculate the yearly dividend payment to the twenty shareholders of the company. The board of directors specified that dividends can be paid only when the cash flow from operations is at least $5,000,000. The owners of the company expect to receive a sizable dividend each year and may fire management if the company fails to produce the required cash flow. On January 15, 2004, Chris and Jeremy calculate the cash flow from operations to be $4,500,000. Their supervisor, Julia Kremer, suggests several ways to increase operating cash flow above the $5,000,000 mark. Her most forceful suggestion is to reclassify a two-year note payable taken out on November 1, 2003, as a current note payable. The change will increase cash flow from operations to $5,250,000 and will permit the payment of the dividend.

Questions

a. Does the reclassification of the long-term note payable to a current liability account have the desired effect on the statement of cash flows? Explain.
b. What is the ethical dilemma described in this problem?
c. Identify parties affected by this reclassification. Who benefits by this change? Who is harmed?
d. What would you do? Explain your answer.
e. How would the situation be changed if the company had borrowed the money on November 1, 2003, as a one-year note payable? If they might have avoided the "dilemma" in the first place by just borrowing the money on a shorter-term note, why can't they simply reclassify the note now, since it is in the company's best interest?

Chapter 4
Corporate Governance

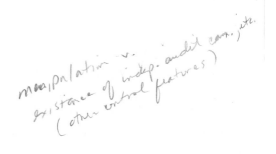

Corporate governance is the term used to describe various ways in which companies regulate themselves or are regulated by their industries or governmental bodies. Such regulation is necessary to ensure that the information available to outsiders represents an unbiased picture of the financial position of the company. Governance issues include efforts to maintain or reestablish the independence of boards of directors (for example, to mandate the election or appointment of outside directors). Governance issues for both for-profit and not-for-profit corporations are considered in this section. In a general fashion, governance encompasses many reform efforts that are intended to support company decisions that support the mission of the company and encourage the disclosure of adequate and accurate financial information to outsider users of that information.

Problems related to corporate governance are presented in three categories: (1) company expenditures; (2) independence issues and corporate decisions; and (3) company pension plans.

COMPANY EXPENDITURES

Case 4.1
Tyco International Ltd.

Tyco International, based in Bermuda, is a manufacturing and service company that sells and maintains electrical components, circuit boards, undersea cable systems, fire detection systems, electronic security systems, special valves, and medical supplies.[1] Total revenue was $30.7 billion for the year ending September 30, 2000, and $36.4 billion for the year ending September 30, 2001. Net income for the year ending September 30, 2000, was $4.5 billion, and net income for the year ending September 30, 2001, was $4.7 billion.

In September 2002, Tyco International filed a report with the SEC alleging that the former CEO, Dennis L. Kozlowski, "misused company funds" for his personal benefit.[2] The funds improperly diverted to Kozlowski and other company executives were in the form of forgiven loans, company payments for real estate, charitable donations, and company payments for personal expenses. The company said the expenditures, totaling over $135 million, occurred for at least five years before Kozlowski's June 3, 2002, resignation.[3] At a time when Kozlowski was publicly supporting high standards of corporate governance, he was privately raiding Tyco's funds to cover his lavish lifestyle and charitable commitments.

Dennis Kozlowski was hired by Tyco in 1976 and became CEO of the company in 1992. When he became CEO in 1992, Tyco was a company with $3 billion in annual sales from sprinklers and packaging materials. Total payroll expense was $14 million. Kozlowski, who grew up in Newark, New Jersey, was determined to increase the size of the company. Within five years, revenue had more than doubled. In 1997, Tyco merged with ADT Ltd., the world's largest supplier of security systems. ADT was registered in Bermuda. Tyco became one of the first U.S. companies to register itself as an offshore company to avoid paying U.S. taxes.

Mr. Kozlowski was paid $9.3 million in salary after the ADT merger was completed. In 1998, his salary was $24 million, with another $41 million in stock options. Tyco developed a retirement program that would give him $4.1 million per year for life, after the age of 65. Kozlowski was paid a total of $400 million in salary and options from 1998–2001.

In addition to his salary and stock options, Mr. Kozlowski used Tyco funds for personal expenditures. These expenditures include the purchase of a house in North Kent, Massachusetts ($15 million); a Boca Raton, Florida, estate purchased with a $19 million loan from Tyco which was later forgiven; the purchase of a second home in Boca Raton to use during the construction of the estate ($2.5 million); the purchase of a Manhattan apartment ($18 million), plus $11 million for furnishings; an art collection worth $13.1 million; charitable donations for athletic facilities for his daughter's school ($1.7 million); a $5 million donation for a building at Seton Hall University from where he graduated in 1968, and a total of $35 million to his favorite local charities—given in his name, but with Tyco's money. He also spent $1.05 million for a fortieth-birthday party for his wife, and purchased racing yachts to support his yachting hobby. *Wall Street Journal* reporters describe Mr. Kozlowski's actions as an attempt "to transfer massive sums of wealth to himself at the expense of shareholders."[4]

In June 2002, Dennis Kozlowski was indicted on tax evasion charges. The indictment charged that he evaded more than $1 million in New York taxes on the purchase of $13 million in artwork. Kozlowski resigned from Tyco and pleaded not guilty to the tax evasion charges. Prosecutors said he purchased art and had it shipped to Tyco headquarters in Exeter, New Hampshire, instead of his New York apartment to avoid paying New York city and state sales tax (8.25 percent).[5]

The allegations that Kozlowski used a "public company as his personal cash machine" raise questions about the oversight function of the board of directors. Unfortunately, the board is composed of company insiders and members with questionable financial dealings of their own, including that of Mark Swartz, chief financial officer, whose $16 million real estate loan from the company was forgiven in 2000.

Questions

a. Describe the ethical dilemma presented in this scenario. Was there a blurring of interests between Tyco and Kozlowski? What did Kozlowski do that was wrong?

b. Identify the parties interested in Kozlowski's personal expenditure of $135 million in company funds.

c. Was Kozlowski entitled to live well because under his directions the company was doing very well? If so, did he have the right to use company funds in the manner he did? Give your reasons.

d. The stock price of Tyco reacted strongly to the news of Kozlowski's lavish lifestyle and expenditures. What do you think the reasons for this were?

e. Why did Kozlowski resign from his job? Who benefited and/or was harmed by this action?

f. What type of oversight should the Tyco board of directors have exercised with regard to these expenditures? Who was harmed by its failure to control its CEO's spending?

Case 4.2
General Electric Company

In September 2002, the SEC opened an informal investigation into retirement packages offered by General Electric to former CEO Jack Welch, who retired in 2001.[6] The compensation package, negotiated in 1996, became public information as a result of divorce proceedings between Welch and his wife, Jane. Her divorce filings report an "extraordinary" lifestyle, largely paid for by GE funds, even after his retirement in 2001.[7]

The divorce filing reported that GE paid for country club memberships, family phones and computers in five homes; flowers; wine and maid service; sports tickets to the Red Sox, Yankees, and Knicks games; Wimbledon tickets; and opera tickets; in addition to expenses for autos, many of the costs of a GE-owned apartment in New York City (valued at $80,000 per month), and the use of GE-owned jets valued at $291,865 per month.

SEC regulations required companies to disclose such benefits contracts, but did not specify the disclosure requirements. SEC regulations required companies to disclose the compensation paid to the five highest-paid executives, but do not require companies to disclose the amount paid to retired executives. GE said that the board had approved Welch's retirement package in 1996. The company included a copy of the agreement in its 1996 proxy filing. The contract, according to the GE report, states that Welch will have access for the remainder of his life to company services provided to him prior to retirement, "including access to company aircraft, cars, office, apartments and financial-planning services" plus reimbursement for "reasonable" travel and living expenses.[8]

The SEC requested information from GE regarding the disclosure to shareholders and the public for the executive perks given to Welch. Welch has insisted that all benefits were disclosed, but he has also said that he will give up most of the perks and begin paying GE $2 to $2.5 million per year for the use of the company apartment and company planes. Welch said he would give up the perks, even though he thought they were reasonable at the time of negotiation, to avoid misperception in the current environment of corporate scandal.

Questions

a. Do you believe Welch's retirement package to be reasonable? What factors influence your decision?

b. Where does the money come from that is paid to the executive in the compensation package? Whose money is it, and who is supposed to manage the money for the company's interests? What are other possible uses of this money?

c. Identify the interested parties in the GE–Welch scenario. Who benefits by these large compensation packages? Who is harmed?

d. Should companies be required to disclose the total compensation paid to retired executives (as they are for current executives)? Is there anything wrong when investors gain this information from reports on divorce filings? Should the SEC rules be altered to deal with such situations?

e. If you were an internal accountant responsible for paying these expenses for Welch, would you have a responsibility to oppose such arrangements? Would you be facing an ethical dilemma? Explain.

Case 4.3
Adelphia Communications Corporation

Three members of the Rigas family who started Adelphia Communications were arrested in July 2002 on charges of "looting the company on a massive scale."[9] In September 2002, the three Rigas family members and two company executives were indicted by a federal grand jury on charges they "looted the company out of hundreds of millions of dollars."[10] The case is described as one of the largest ever of alleged insider dealing by company officials. John Rigas, the 78-year-old company founder, and his two sons, Timothy J. Rigas, chief financial officer of the company, and Michael J. Rigas, operations vice president, were charged in the indictment with securities fraud, wire fraud, and bank fraud. The SEC also filed a fraud complaint against Adelphia in July 2002.

The arrests and indictments followed a formal investigation opened by the SEC in April 2002 into Adelphia's "accounting and disclosure practices related to off-balance sheet loans" and the June 3, 2002, action by the Nasdaq to delist Adelphia's stock.[11] This action was taken because Adelphia failed to "timely file its periodic reports with the Securities and Exchange Commission as required by Nasdaq rules and based upon public interest concerns."[12] On June 25, 2002, Adelphia, the sixth-largest cable television company in the United States, filed for Chapter 11 bankruptcy protection which allows a company to continue to operate as it sorts out its financial problems.[13] Creditors asked for "audited, accurate financial statements" for 2001. The 2001 audit was suspended pending the investigation of self-dealing by Adelphia and the Rigas family.

According to the criminal complaint, the "Rigases engaged in a mass cover-up that included fictitious receipts, falsified financial reports and lavish personal spending at the expense of shareholders."[14] The first public announcement of trouble at the company was made in March 2002. Adelphia announced a fourth-quarter loss of $1.33 billion, or $6.95 per share, and reported that they were responsible for $2.3 billion of debt for loans to family-owned entities that were not recorded on the company's balance sheet.

In 1999 the company expanded to keep up with its competitors, Comcast Corporation and AT&T Corporation. As it acquired new companies and doubled its size to more than five million subscribers, it increased its debt load almost four times, from $3.5 to $12.6 billion. Investors and rating agencies were unhappy about the amount of debt on the Adelphia balance sheet and demanded that the company reduce the debt. To comply with this request, the Rigas executives "embarked on a series of escalating financial frauds to conceal the borrowings and inflate earnings,"[15] according to the SEC complaint. At the same time, the family members withdrew large sums of money from the company for their private use. According to Wayne Carlin, regional director of the SEC's Northeast regional office, "The thing that makes this case stand out is the scope and magnitude of the looting of the company on the part of the Rigas family. In terms of the brazenness and the amount of dollars yanked out of this public company and yanked out of the pockets of investors, it's really quite stunning. It's even stunning to someone like me who is in the business of unraveling these kinds of schemes."[16]

According to the complaint, the Rigases used company jets for private vacations, including an African safari, and borrowed billions of dollars from Adelphia for their private use. John Rigas began withdrawing so much money from the company to cover his personal debts that finally his son had to limit him to $1 million per month. Public filings with the SEC list his salary at less than $1.9 million per year, and do not list the $12 million he withdrew, based on his monthly limit.

In 2001–2002, the Rigases reported to shareholders that they were buying company stock to "ease the debt pressures." What they failed to disclose was that they were using Adelphia money to make these purchases. According to the SEC complaint, to make it appear that they were using their own money to buy the stock, Timothy Rigas told Adelphia employees to "create false receipts showing payment by the family for the stock."[17]

Adelphia created false transactions to increase its revenue. In October 2000, Timothy Rigas discovered that the company's ebitda (earnings before interest, taxes, depreciation, and amortization) were less than analysts' forecasts, and he instructed accountants to generate false invoices to increase revenue. This practice continued in 2001, as the company determined "a target number for Adelphia's publicly disclosed Ebitda and would attempt to justify that number by creating back-dated sham transactions"[18] between Adelphia and the other family-owned companies.

In the years 1998–2000, Adelphia reported revenues between $.5 billion and $2.91 billion, yet net income included losses of $89 million to $548 million. By June 2002,

Adelphia disclosed that it had inflated cash flow from 2000 and 2001 by more than $500 million and had boosted its cable-TV subscriber numbers by 50,000. In March 2002, the stock price of the company was $20.39. When the disclosures of the inflated cash flow and subscriber numbers were made, the stock price was $0.70 and subsequently delisted.

All Rigas family members resigned from the board of directors and their management positions in the company in May 2002. In September 2002, Adelphia announced it would not pay John Rigas his $4.2 million severance pay that he had negotiated when he agreed to step down in May.[19]

The SEC is asking for the return of hundreds of millions of dollars including "all ill-gotten gains including—as to the individuals—all compensation received during the fraud, all property unlawfully taken from Adelphia through undisclosed related party transactions, and any severance payments related to their resignations." This case was described as "one of the largest ever of alleged insider dealing by company officials."[20]

Questions

a. Identify the parties affected by the financial fraud. Who benefits? Who is harmed?
b. What accounting principles or concepts did Adelphia violate?
c. Imagine that you are an accountant who was responsible for overseeing these huge payments to the Rigas family members. What might you have done? What kind of pressures might have been brought to bear on you?
d. What might have been the impact of falsifying subscriber numbers on potential investors? Explain your answer.
e. What role should have been played by the board of directors as the Rigas family was diverting company funds for their private use? What could the board of directors have done to become aware of these transactions?

Case 4.4
Travel and Entertainment Expense for a Not-for-profit Company

A recent article in a newspaper described several questionable business practices in a not-for-profit insurance company. A state audit had documented questionable spending for executives' travel and annual board retreats at a resort. The chief executive of the insurance company said that steps had been taken to correct the deficiencies noted in the audit. He apologized for several other actions, including a business trip to Hawaii where he billed the insurance company for $800 for a helicopter ride. The executive defended the board's annual retreats as educational, but he agreed that the expenditures for cocktails, golf, and golf lessons for board members and their families might not have been reasonable expenditures for a not-for-profit insurance company.

Questions

a. What is the ethical dilemma involving the not-for-profit organization that is discussed in this article?

b. The chief executive stated that corrective steps had been taken, including new policies regarding travel and entertainment expenses. If the new policy regarding travel expenses is to be an effective internal control, what procedures might guard against error? Identify three. (Consider the general characteristics of an effective control system.)

c. Would these expenses have been questioned if the insurance company operated as a for-profit enterprise? What are the key distinctions in the two types of insurance companies that may affect the way expenses might be treated?

d. During the interview a reporter asked the executive if it was fair that his company was held to different standards than were for-profit insurance companies. What issue is the reporter raising? If you were a chief executive officer in this position, what might you say to the reporter? Do you think standards for these two types of companies should differ?

Case 4.5
Business Expenditures for a Not-for-profit Company

Dan Green has been working on the audit of a not-for-profit residential treatment facility for mentally disturbed teenagers. Dan is an employee of one of the big four audit firms. He is a second year auditor, and this particular engagement is the first audit where he is in charge of the fieldwork. He is currently reviewing the working papers of the assistant working with him, in preparation for the manager's visit next week. The audit has gone well, and the audit team is currently reviewing invoices for expense items related to the audit of the income statement. Dan has just uncovered several invoices that are puzzling to him, including an invoice for yacht insurance, several invoices for lavish entertainment expenses, including cigars and food in connection with a conference in Chicago; invoices for expensive clothing purchased as gifts for the directors of the organization; and invoices for oriental rugs for the house provided to the director of the facility. Since there is no body of water large enough to support a yacht within hundreds of miles of the facility, Dan feels he must question the accounting staff about this expenditure. According to the controller, the yacht is moored off the coast of California and is used by the director to entertain friends.

Questions

a. What is the ethical dilemma described in this problem?
b. Identify the interested parties to the decision. Who benefits? Who is harmed?
c. What alternatives are available to Dan?
d. What would you do?

e. How would your answer change if the facility were operating as a for-profit institution? Does the distinction between the two types of institutions justify alternative approaches to the financial reporting?

INDEPENDENCE ISSUES AND CORPORATE DECISIONS

Case 4.6
Collecting Donations

As the controller for Smith-Johnson College, you are reviewing the results of the latest fund drive, designed to raise $100 million for state-of-the-art classrooms for the business department. You were pleased with the results of the fund drive two years ago when the pledges were made, but the actual cash payments have been very slow in the last year. Because you used the pledges to guarantee the loan on the building, you now have a dilemma. The cash flow is not adequate to make the loan payments. The vice president of finance has suggested filing a lawsuit against the donors for breach of contract. You are not sure whether you want to file a lawsuit against the donors, some of whom are your friends, even though the college is about to become delinquent on its loan payments. It seems to you that filing suit against the donors for nonpayment of their pledges is not a very charitable action for a not-for-profit organization. It will be difficult to raise money in the next fund drive if the word gets out that Smith-Johnson will sue a donor who doesn't meet a pledge promptly. Yet the college does have a responsibility to protect its assets, and the loan payments must be made to prevent foreclosure on the building by the lending institution.

Questions

a.   What is the ethical dilemma described in this problem?
b.   Identify the interested parties involved in this situation. Who benefits? Who is harmed?
c.   What options are available to the controller?
d.   Does your knowledge of GAAP help you resolve this dilemma? Why?
e.   What would you do? Justify your position.

Case 4.7
The Vanguard Group, Inc.

Vanguard, the second-largest mutual fund company in the United States, with holdings of about $300 billion in stocks, has taken a more active role in corporate governance. In a letter to leaders of the companies where Vanguard holds a major stake, Vanguard said it would take the following actions in regard to proxy votes:

(1)   *Director Independence.* Vanguard will not vote for nonindependent directors who serve on audit, compensation, or nominating committees. It will also withhold votes for any director whose election would make the majority of a company's board made up of insiders (these rules are consistent with the independence rules issued by the New York Stock Exchange, although the NYSE has given companies two years to comply).

(2) *Auditor Independence.* Vanguard will vote against the company's independent auditor if non-audit fees make up more than 50 percent of the fees paid to the auditor.

(3) *Stock Option Plans.* Vanguard will vote against stock option plans if potential dilution from the plan exceeds 15 percent of shares outstanding or if shares granted on annual option grants exceed 2 percent of the shares outstanding.

Questions

a. How do the changes in proxy voting made by Vanguard improve corporate governance?

b. Will these changes have an impact on the corporate governance structures used by corporations?

c. Do you agree with the changes adopted by Vanguard?

Case 4.8
Walt Disney Company

The New York Stock Exchange (NYSE) has established corporate governance standards for the board of directors for companies selling stock on the stock exchange. These guidelines specify that a director will not be considered independent if an immediate family member has worked for the company in the previous five years. Walt Disney Company currently has thirteen independent board members and three nonindependent board members. Three of the board members considered to be independent will not be independent under the new rules, including the chairman of the corporate governance and nominating committee, the chairman of the audit and compensation committee, and a member of the audit and compensation committee. These three board members have adult children who are either currently working for the company or who have been employed at the company in the past year. New board members will be selected for the committee positions.

Questions

a. Describe the conflicts of interest of a board member who is not independent.

b. How might the changes in the board membership improve corporate governance at Walt Disney Company?

c. Identify the stakeholders who benefit by this change. Which stakeholders are harmed?

COMPANY PENSION PLANS

Case 4.9
Lucent Technologies

Lockdowns v. g/l in stock val
v. governance weakness/strength

D. Pela Resa

Lucent employees watched their company stock plummet when Lucent announced it would miss its fourth-quarter estimated earnings. Due to a 15-day lockdown, employees who were members of the company's 401(k) plan were prohibited from making changes in their asset allocations during the announced lockdown period.

On October 10, 2000, Lucent issued a press release indicating it would miss the analysts' estimate of its fourth-quarter EPS.[21] On October 11, the price of Lucent stock fell 32 percent to $21.25. But the 114,000 Lucent employees who were members of the company's 401(k) savings plan could not sell their stock at that time because Fidelity Investments, the plan administrator, needed time to balance the assets of the pension plan after a spin-off of one of the subsidiaries. (It is legal for a company to prohibit employees from selling company stock during a lockdown period. According to a company spokesperson, on any business day, 96 company plans out of 350,000 companies that have 401(k) plans are in a lockdown.)

Paul Rinderele, a 65-year-old retiree of AT&T, said he lost $10,000 on his Lucent stock in a day. Lucent said that employees had plenty of time to sell their stock before the lockdown. They were notified several times that the lockdown would occur. Previous earnings warnings had already caused Lucent stock to fall from $77 at the beginning of 2000 to $27.01 at the beginning of the lockdown period. To this date, no legal proceedings have been filed regarding Rinderele and his fellow pensioners.

Questions

a. Is it legal for a company to prohibit employees from selling company stock during a lockdown period?
b. Even if this is legal, is a stock lockdown ethical? Explain your answers. Is anyone harmed?
c. What is the employee's responsibility for making stock purchase decisions in a 401(k) plan? Should employees have sold their company stock before the lockdown? Are they right to blame the company for the decline in value that occurred during the lockdown?

Case 4.10
Enron Corporation

Enron, a company formed by the merger of energy companies in Texas and Nebraska, specialized in producing natural gas. In the early 1990s, Enron began to diversify into energy marketing and high-band communications. Enron's stock price rose rapidly from

$43 per share in January 1997 to $90 per share by August 2000. By February 2002, however, the stock had fallen to $0.40 per share.

Enron employees were encouraged to purchase company stock for their 401(k) retirement funds. Even as the stock price fell, Kenneth Lay, the chairman of Enron, told employees to buy more company stock. At the same time Lay sold his own Enron shares worth $29.8 million.

As the news about Enron's financial problems began to surface, Enron employees were locked out of selling the Enron stock in their pension plan. During the lockdown period (from October 26, 2001, to November 13, 2001), the price of Enron stock dropped from $15.40 to $9.98. The lockdown occurred because Enron switched pension plan administrators. Charlie Prestwood, a retired Enron employee, watched the $1.2 million value of Enron stock in his retirement plan fall to a value of $5,300.[22] At the time of the lockdown, the Enron retirement plans had about 11,000 participants and held about $1.3 billion of assets, including $1 billion of Enron stock purchase directly by employees.

Questions

a. Identify the parties affected by the Enron decision to change pension plan administrators at the end of November. What parties benefit? What parties are harmed?

b. What responsibility do Enron employees have to select stocks for their 401(k) pension plans? Are they justified in blaming Enron for their bad investment decisions?

c. What should Mr. Prestwood have done with his 401(k) stock? Is it appropriate for him to blame CEO Kenneth Lay and Enron for his pension plan losses?

Endnotes

[1] *"Key facts for Tyco International Ltd.," The Wall Street Journal,* September 19, 2002.

[2] "Tyco accuses Kozlowski, others of illegal actions," *The Wall Street Journal,* September 17, 2002.

[3] Mark Maremont and Laurie P. Cohen, "Tyco spent millions for benefit of Kozlowski, its former CEO," *The Wall Street Journal,* August 7, 2002.

[4] Mark Maremont and Laurie P. Cohen, "Tyco spent millions for benefit of Kozlowski," its Former CEO," *The Wall Street Journal,* August 8, 2002.

[5] David Armstrong, "Former Tyco executive moves to dismiss tax-evasion charges," *The Wall Street Journal,* August 29, 2002.

[6] "SEC investigates package that GE offered to Welch," *The Wall Street Journal,* September 16, 2002.

[7] Matt Murray, JoAnn Lublin, and Rachel Emma Silverman, "Welch's lavish retirement package angers General Electric investors," *The Wall Street Journal,* September 9, 2002.

[8] Ibid.

[9] Jerry Markon and Robert Frank, "Adelphia officials are arrested, charged with 'massive' fraud," *The Wall Street Journal,* July 25, 2002.

[10] "Federal grand jury indicts former Adelphia executives," *The Wall Street Journal*, September 23, 2002.

[11] Rober Frank, "SEC opens a formal investigation into cable firm Adelphia's finances," *The Wall Street Journal,* April 18, 2002.

[12] Deborah Solomon and Robert Frank, "Nasdaq plans to delist Adelphia, triggering clause in bond deal," *The Wall Street Journal*, May 31, 2002.

[13] Deborah Solomon, "Adelphia files for chapter 11; financing to keep it operable," *The Wall Street Journal*, June 26, 2002.

[14] Jerry Markon and Robert Frank, "Adelphia officials are arrested, charged with 'massive' fraud," *The Wall Street Journal,* July 25, 2002.

[15] Ibid.

[16] Ibid.

[17] Ibid.

[18] Ibid.

[19] Dinah Wisenberg Brin, "Adelphia decides not to pay Rigas $4.2 million severance," *The Wall Street Journal,* September 11, 2002.

[20] "Federal grand jury indicts former Adelphia executives," *The Wall Street Journal*, September 23, 2002.

[21] Dennis K. Berman, "Accounting for Enron: All tied up: Retirement-plan lockdowns at Lucent and elsewhere draw questions," *The Wall Street Journal,* January 21, 2002.

[22] Richard Willing, "Odds workers will receive Enron payoff: 'Slim'; 401(k) holders are the last to recover losses under bankruptcy law," *USA Today,* February 4, 2002.

Chapter 5
Financial Statement Reporting and Disclosure

In the contemporary environment where financial forecasts by Wall Street analysts and the pressure of stock prices influence companies to hide financial information that may reflect negatively on their performance, appropriate disclosure in press releases and in financial statements remains a high priority. Companies often attempt to prevent outsiders from discovering information that suggests poor performance or less favorable performance than that projected by analysts. In times of volatile stock prices, failure to meet analysts' forecasts often has exaggerated negative consequences (declining stock prices), and companies find themselves disclosing information that suggests growth from year to year. In these expressions of bias toward company growth, news releases often will include pro forma earnings that do not meet accounting practice standards. These reports may mislead outsiders, including investors and those who are considering loans to the company. In this context, management may sometimes disclose nonrecurring items as if they are not the responsibility of management.

Problems related to financial statement reporting and disclosure are presented in three categories: (1) financial statement disclosure; (2) proforma reports and press releases; and (3) footnote and supplemental disclosures.

FINANCIAL STATEMENT DISCLOSURE

Case 5.1
Enron Corporation

On October 16, 2001, Enron, the nation's largest marketer of electricity and natural gas, reported $638 million in losses and a $1.2 billion reduction in shareholder equity.[1] The SEC opened an inquiry into Enron's related party transactions on October 22, 2001. This inquiry was elevated to a formal investigation on October 31, 2001. On November 8, 2001, Enron restated its financial statements for 1997–2000, slashing $586 million (20 percent) from profit to account for losses over a four-year period.

On November 8, 2001, the SEC issued a subpoena to Arthur Andersen related to the Enron audit. Arthur Andersen, the auditor for Enron and one of the Big Five auditing firms, was an 89-year-old firm with 2001 revenue of $9.3 billion, 85,000 employees in 84 countries, and 2,300 public clients. On November 29, 2001 Standard & Poor's lowered Enron's credit rating to junk status, an action that meant that $3.9 billion of debt became due. On December 2, 2001, Enron filed for bankruptcy and fired 4,500 employees (about one-fourth of its workforce).

Enron, the nation's seventh-largest corporation, is headquartered in Houston, Texas. The company transports natural gas through pipelines in the United States and generates and distributes electricity to markets in the Northwest. Prior to the bankruptcy filing, Enron had 20,600 employees. More than 87 percent of the employees left the company after the bankruptcy announcement. Financial information for the company is provided below.

Year	Revenue (in billions)	Net Income (in billions)
1998	$ 31.0	$ 0.70
1999	$ 40.1	$ 1.02
2000	$100.8	$ 0.98

The stock, at $90 was at its peak in August 2000, increasing by 55 percent in 1999 and 87 percent in 2000.[2] By October 2001, the stock price had dropped to about $35 per share. By December 2001, when Enron filed for bankruptcy, the stock had fallen to less than $1 per share. The stock was thereafter delisted.

In January 2002, Enron fired its auditor, Arthur Andersen, and Arthur Andersen fired David Duncan, the partner in charge of the Enron audit. In March 2002, Arthur Andersen was indicted by federal prosecutors for destroying Enron-related documents. The "obstruction of justice" criminal trial against Arthur Andersen began in Houston on May 6, 2002. On June 15, 2002, Arthur Andersen was convicted of a single count of obstruction of justice. As a result of the felony conviction, Arthur Andersen was prevented from auditing publicly owned clients. The firm announced it would cease audit filings for public clients as of August 31, 2002. The Big Five accounting firms had become the Big Four.

Arthur Andersen and Enron were brought down because of the actions of a few individuals within the companies. The companies allowed these actions to flourish because the "tone at the top" of the organizations was bad; that is, company executives encouraged deception, fostered a "win at any price" attitude, and deliberately ignored the interests of their own employees and outside investors. Enron sought profit without disclosure. Arthur Andersen allowed conflicts of interest between its "watch guard" audit function and its goal of generating revenue from its second-largest audit client through consulting fees. The case of Enron and Arthur Andersen is an example of a massive failure of corporate oversight systems, including the auditor, company executives, Wall Street analysts, credit-rating agencies, company directors, and banks.

The Auditors

On August 31, 2002, Arthur Andersen surrendered its license to practice accounting in all fifty states. This action was taken as a result of its June 2002 felony conviction for obstruction of justice during the Enron investigation. The jury conviction came after ten days of jury deliberation. The jury agreed that at least one individual in the firm, Nancy

Temple, an Arthur Andersen attorney, had attempted to get audit work paper documents altered to protect the firm from SEC scrutiny. The audit papers that were altered related to a memo written by the audit partner, David Duncan, concerning the news release for the third-quarter Enron earnings. Duncan wrote in the memo that the information in the press release "could potentially be misunderstood by investors." In the press release, Enron had reported $1.01 billion of nonrecurring charges and said that the company was "on track" to meet its earnings targets in 2002. Enron released the press release, despite the concerns of the audit partner concerning the misleading information in the release. Nancy Temple, an Arthur Andersen lawyer, advised David Duncan to change the memo to protect the firm from SEC scrutiny.

Arthur Andersen had been the auditor for Enron since the company was formed in 1985 through the merger of two companies. Enron was Andersen's second-largest audit client, generating audit fees, including internal and external, of about $25 million per year and consulting fees, including tax and consulting services, of about $27 million per year. Andersen had performed internal audit services for Enron since the early 1990s. Accounting firms that perform internal and external audit work for a client normally try to prevent conflicts of interest between the two groups, but Arthur Andersen encouraged their audit and consulting groups to work together, giving both groups office space on the same floor at Enron.

Andersen auditors developed close ties with Enron. An Andersen marketing videotape was prepared, using the Enron audit as an example of its integrated audit approach that combined the external audit role with the internal audit role. Andersen also provided consulting services within this integrated approach. The Andersen auditors were on site at Enron for the entire year, rather than merely during the interim and year-end audit periods. An Enron employee, interviewed for a marketing videotape, said, "We expect them to be here and to be able to be responsive to our needs…hopefully even being able to reach the conclusion we want."

Interested parties outside Enron and Andersen wonder what went wrong. If Andersen was hired by Enron to protect the interests of outsiders, why did Andersen act like an Enron employee? Andersen helped Enron set up the off-balance sheet partnerships that hid Enron debt. Andersen auditors knew about the partnerships and the debt they held, but the firm continued to bend to the wishes of Enron executives who wanted to keep the losses off the Enron books. Andersen auditors asked for advice regarding the correct accounting for Enron transactions but failed to follow the advice received from the Professional Standards Group at Andersen. In 1997, Enron failed to record audit adjustments proposed by Andersen, and the firm determined that the adjustments were "immaterial" even though they added up to nearly half of Enron's net income.

Company Executives and the Board of Directors

Enron executives kept billions of dollars of debt off their balance sheet by using special-purpose entities (SPEs). According to a report commissioned by the board of directors, Enron used at least fifty SPEs for financing transactions. The report examined only six transactions for a few SPEs, occurring during 1997–2001. These six transactions provided Enron with $1.38 billion in cash and "had dramatic effects on both the balance sheet and income statement portions of Enron's financial statements."[3] The report continued, "Enron was prolific in its use of highly complex structured finance transactions using SPEs, with the results that billions of dollars of recourse obligations were not disclosed as debt in Enron's balance sheet, and the proceeds of these recourse obligations were reported as revenue and cash flow." In the transactions, Enron "supposedly" sold an asset to the SPE in exchange for cash. The SPE often borrowed money to pay Enron. The SPEs were held by partnerships that were run by Enron executives. When the partnerships were added to the Enron books as a result of the restatement announced in October 2001, hundreds of millions of dollars of debt were added to the balance sheet.

Senior level executives at Enron received large bonuses, including $744 million in salary, bonuses, and stock grants paid to 140 executives (an average of $5.3 million each) before the bankruptcy filing. The company had been paying large bonuses to executives for many years, some of them related to earning performance and increases in stock prices; thus providing an incentive for executives to misstate financial reports. Business commentators have coined the phrase "feeding at the corporate trough" to describe the business practice of removing money from the corporation in the form of bonus payments. For example, between February and October of 2001, Kenneth Lay (the CEO of Enron) sold $90.1 million of company stock even while he was advising company employees to buy additional shares of Enron stock.

Enron's board of directors waived their code of corporate ethics twice in 1999 to allow two outside partnerships to be run by Andrew Fastow, the CFO of Enron. Fastow had a financial interest in the partnerships and consequently made more than $30 million from them. The board notes say that Fastow's participation in the partnerships "will not adversely affect the interests of the company." Because the ethics code violations were waived by the board, the insurance carriers for the directors' coverage are trying to limit their liability.

Wall Street Analysts, Credit-Rating Agencies, and Banks

Wall Street Analysts loved Enron stock because it consistently beat earnings forecasts. Ten of fifteen analysts who followed Enron rated the stock as a "buy" or "strong buy" as late as November 8, 2001, several weeks after the SEC announced its investigation of the company's financial situation. A First Bank analyst also rated Enron "a strong buy" as late as November 29, 2001, three days before the bankruptcy filing.

Enron debt was also rated favorable by credit-rating agencies. Late in October 2001, Moody's and Standard & Poor's gave Enron a solid investment grade rating. Critics wonder if credit rating agencies waited a little too long to downgrade Enron debt, since the debt had already dropped in value in the market. The credit-rating agencies finally responded to the market price of Enron debt by lowering the company's credit rating to "junk" status on November 28, 2001. As soon as the debt was lowered to junk status, $3.9 billion of debt became immediately due. Enron filed for bankruptcy four days later.

Large banking institutions extended loans to the Enron off-balance sheets partnerships to finance the special-purpose entities. These loans were structured by the banks in ways that allowed Enron to record the cash as coming from trades rather than loans. This helped improve the firm's operating cash flow so it matched the company's paper profits. Citigroup, the nation's largest financial institution, and J.P. Morgan Chase & Co. made more than $200 million in fees from structuring these transactions. The SEC is investigating Citigroup and J.P. Morgan to determine whether the banks helped Enron hide debt and increase cash flow. Senate investigators are also examining the involvement of Enron's bankers: "It has become common knowledge that Enron engaged in accounting deceptions to convince lenders, investors and analysts that the company was in better financial shape than it was."[4]

Questions

a. Identify the ethical dilemma for the auditors.

b. Do you believe it is fair that Arthur Andersen was put out of business by the actions of just one audit partner in Houston, Texas? Because of his actions, the Arthur Andersen office in Europe, Asia, and in every state in the United States closed. Explain the action taken by Arthur Andersen that resulted in the closing of the company.

c. Arthur Andersen sold their consulting practice many years ago, yet they reported $27 million in consulting fees for Enron. If the consulting practice was sold, what is the source of the consulting fees? Is this action ethical on the part of auditing firms?

d. Outside regulators propose that auditing firms should be prevented from performing consulting services to avoid conflicts of interest. Many auditing firms, including Arthur Andersen, have sold their consulting practices. Did the sale of the consulting practice by Arthur Andersen allow the company to avoid conflicts of interest in the Enron case? Explain your answer.

e. David Duncan, the partner in charge of the Enron audit, has been described as a "nice guy" who in a business meeting would not want to disagree with anyone. As a shareholder of the company, would you be happy with this description of the audit partner in charge of protecting your interests? What "interested party" would be happy with the description of David Duncan?

f. Most of the auditing firms in the United States are structured as limited liability partnerships (LLP) or limited liability corporations (LLC). In the case of Enron, describe the liability of the Arthur Andersen partnership and David Duncan in regard to lawsuits filed against the company for the audit failure at Enron.

g. Was it appropriate for Arthur Andersen to provide consulting, external auditing, and internal auditing services for Enron? Did Arthur Andersen behave ethically? What section of the professional code of conduct did they violate by their behavior?

h. Does it appear that Andersen maintained an "independence in appearance" position with Enron? Should auditors become employees of the companies they audit, as the Andersen marketing videotape described the relationship between Andersen and Enron? And then if they do, should they brag about it?

i. Did Nancy Temple act ethically when she advised David Duncan to alter the memo in the Enron file to avoid the suggestion that the client's financial information was misleading?

j. During the obstruction of justice trial, Arthur Andersen was accused of shredding Enron workpapers. Did Andersen act ethically when they destroyed evidence relating to the Enron audit? Why do you think the jury was bothered by the shredding?

k. Did Arthur Andersen act ethically when they passed audit adjustments equal to 50 percent of net income in 1997? How could an audit firm justify this decision?

l. Did Andersen act ethically when they helped Enron set up the partnerships for the off-balance sheet debt? Did they violate any accounting standard or principle? If so, identify this standard or principle.

m. Did the top executives at Enron act ethically when they set up the partnerships to keep debt off their books? What incentive did they have to act in this fashion?

n. Is "feeding at the corporate trough" ethical behavior? Identify the parties harmed by this behavior. Which parties benefit?

o. Did Kenneth Lay act ethically when he advised employees to purchase Enron stock at the same time he was selling his stock? Why did he take this action?

p. Did Wall Street analysts act ethically when they advised investors to purchase Enron stock, even when there were signs of financial problems? What incentive did the analysts have to report favorably on Enron stock?

q. Did credit rating agencies act ethically in rating Enron's credit? What incentives do credit rating agencies have to delay downgrading a company's credit rating?

r. Did the banks act ethically in lending money to the Enron partnerships? What incentive did they have to provide financing for the partnerships?

Case 5.2
Raytheon, SEC Investigation of Disclosure Regulation

Raytheon, the fourth-largest defense contractor in the United States, negotiated with the SEC to settle charges that the company failed to publicly disclose financial information before discussing it with Wall Street analysts.[5] They were charged with violating SEC Regulation FD for "fair disclosure." The rule, which became effective in October 2000, was intended to end the long-standing corporate practice of providing financial information that might have an impact on stock price to Wall Street analysts, giving the analysts and their institutional investors an edge over smaller investors. Under the provisions of Regulation FD, all investors must receive "meaningful financial information" at the same time.

The SEC probe, which began in March 2001, focused on whether Frank Caine, the chief financial officer of Raytheon, violated Regulation FD when he held a series of conversations with Wall Street analysts. Raytheon denied any wrongdoing, saying that the conversations with analysts did not disclose any new information that should have been publicly released. The SEC interviewed more than twelve Wall Street analysts in building its case. After the interviews, the SEC voted to bring an enforcement action against Raytheon, and the SEC ended its probe.

Questions

a.   Describe the rationale for Regulation FD.
b.   Identify the interested parties affected by the Raytheon disclosure. Who benefits from the disclosure? Who is harmed?
c.   What advice would you give Frank Caine if he were about to hold a phone conference with Wall Street analysts on this matter?
d.   Some students of Wall Street claim that "institutional investors always have an advantage over smaller investors," so actions like Raytheon's are not important enough to worry about. What do you think of this view of such actions?

Case 5.3
Interpublic Groups, Earnings Restatements

Interpublic Groups, one of the world's largest advertising holding companies, restated five years of earnings after discovering $68.5 million in expenses that had not been properly recorded.[6] The advertising agency, McCann-Erickson Europe, had failed to reconcile its intercompany accounts on a timely basis. Interpublic had to lower its annual profits for 1997–2000 by amounts ranging from $4 million to $6.8 million per year. The net loss for 2001 increased by $5.9 million.

Business writers speculate the companies are carefully reviewing their financial results because of an SEC requirement that chief executives and finance chiefs swear under oath in writing that the numbers in their corporations' financial filings are correct. Interpublic said that its executives intend to comply with the SEC requirement.

Questions

a.   Who are the interested parties to the SEC requirement that business executives certify financial results? Who benefits? Who is harmed by this requirement?
b.   Might the SEC requirement improve the quality of information available to outside decision makers? As a result of the SEC requirement, might the information be more useful to interested parties? Explain your answers.

Case 5.4
General Electric, Annual Report

General Electric Company's 2001 annual report is 93 pages in length and contains 30 precent more financial information than the 2000 report.[7] General Electric had promised greater disclosure in financial reporting as news of the Enron scandal hit the business newspapers, saying that its annual report would be as big as the New York City phone book if that is what it took to satisfy investors.

In the annual report, General Electric included a special section about its use of "special-purpose entities." Many companies, including Enron and General Electric, use special-purpose entities as a means of off-balance sheet financing. General Electric, however, provided very specific information to distinguish its use of special-purpose entities from Enron's. In the annual report the company said that none of its special-purpose entities was permitted to hold General Electric stock, that the "entities do not engage in speculation activities of any description, and no General Electric employee is permitted to invest in any sponsored special purpose entity."

Wall Street analysts welcomed General Electric's extensive reporting, saying that, "GE has definitely raised the bar for all corporate reporting."[8]

Questions

a. Identify the interested parties in General Electric's new disclosure policy. Who benefits? Who is harmed?
b. In the modern corporate environment, what factors ought to shape a company's decision about the extent of its financial disclosure in the annual report? (Who uses the report? Should the decision focus on shareholders, stock price, "outsiders"?)
c. Is more disclosure always better? (What are the benefits to the company? What are the costs?)
d. Has the bar has been raised for financial disclosure? Explain your answer.
e. Is the extent of disclosure an ethical issue? How might you determine the extent of a company's disclosure? Might your answer be different if you were an internal accountant rather than, for example, an auditor examining a client's books? (Discuss potential sources of bias, the principle of neutrality.)

Case 5.5
Boston Chicken

In 1995, the SEC received an anonymous report that the financial statements of Boston Chicken did not disclose the correct amount of risk assumed by the company for restaurants that were franchised.[9] On the advice of its auditor, Arthur Andersen, Boston Chicken had not consolidated the operating results of its franchisees. Andersen memos show that the auditors reviewed the accounting rules for consolidation and the SEC requirements and decided that they could keep the losses off the books for the company. According to an Andersen memo, this choice of accounting methods fell in a "somewhat grey" area, but was "defendable." The memos reflect no discussion of the information available to investors if the losses were kept off the books.

The company used franchisees to open more than 1,000 restaurants from 1992–1997, loaning them as much as 80 percent of their capital. The franchisees paid license and royalty fees, as well as debt services, to the parent. Loan payments from the franchisees to the parent company were booked by Boston Chicken as revenue. An anonymous letter claimed that Boston Chicken's financial reports did not "disclose the level of risk that I have seen first hand." This apparently refers to the fact that many franchisees suffered losses and there was a probability that many franchisees would not be profitable. These affiliates' losses might have been more fully disclosed by Boston Chicken in its financial statements.

Under accounting rules, Boston Chicken should have reviewed loans periodically to provide an allowance for uncollectible loans, listing some loans as impaired. In addition, prior to 1996, the franchisees' losses were not recorded on the parent company books. In 1996, the SEC required Boston Chicken to report the total losses of its franchisees and consolidate the results of its books. In the SEC filing, Boston Chicken listed losses for the franchisees of $9.8 million in 1993, $47 million in 1994, and $149.1 million in 1995. By the end of 1997, Boston Chicken should have listed more than $630 million in impaired loans from the franchisees. In each year, the franchisees' losses exceeded the net income that had been reported by Boston Chicken. Arthur Andersen, Boston Chicken's audit firm, defended the company and said the disclosures were adequate.

Boston Chicken filed for bankruptcy in 1998. The company was purchased by McDonald's Corporation in 2000 and continues to operate under the name Boston Market. Andersen agreed to pay $10.3 million in February 2002 to settle a shareholder lawsuit regarding the firm's collapse. Boston Chicken creditors lost more than $1 billion following the bankruptcy filing.

Investigators suggest that the Boston Chicken case is an example of how auditors can help clients follow the letter, but not the spirit, of the law, at the expense of investors.

Questions

a. Is the anonymous letter correct in its claim of how Boston Chicken should have handled the reporting of its franchisees' loans?
b. In February 2002, Andersen paid $10.3 million to settle a shareholder's suit alleging "flawed audits." How might Andersen have erred in the matter of the loans and losses?
c. The anonymous letter claimed that Boston Chicken was "hiding risk." In your opinion, was this the case? Give reasons.
d. Did Boston Chicken "faithfully represent" its economic situation? Should the franchisees' losses have been recorded in the Boston Chicken books?

e. Why did the auditors fail to consider the investors in their choice of accounting methods?

f. Does the auditor act ethically when considering whether an accounting choice is defendable?

g. Do you agree that Arthur Andersen followed the "letter, but not the spirit" of the accounting rules in this situation?

Case 5.6
Adelphia, Disclosure of Debt in Financial Statements

An SEC lawsuit alleged that Adelphia officials "fraudulently excluded from the company's annual and quarterly consolidated financial statements over $2.3 billion in bank debt by shifting them onto the books" of their unconsolidated affiliate (controlled by Rigas family members who also founded and at that time played significant roles in Adelphia).[10]

The SEC also alleged that Adelphia financial reports published a series of misrepresentations, including the creation of "sham transactions backed by fictitious documents" to give the "false appearance" that Adelphia had actually repaid debts…" and that Adelphia made "misleading financial statements by giving the false impression through use of footnotes that liabilities listed in the financial statements included all outstanding bank debt."[11] Apparently for these transactions, members of the Rigas family were in critical decision-making committees for authorizing the loans that affiliates received.

Questions

a. If such transactions were made by Adelphia, why were they significant enough to draw the attention of SEC investigators? (Who might have benefited? Who might have been harmed by such transactions?)

b. Why might the SEC criticize the corporate structures that approved the loans?

c. If Rigas family members "drew down" a portion of these loans and used the money for their private purchase of company stock and other properties, what principle of corporate responsibility on the part of executives may have been violated?

d. Should Adelphia's board of directors and its auditor have criticized these transactions? Give reasons for your answer.

Case 5.7
Adelphia, Earnings Reports

The SEC accused Adelphia Communications Corporation of inflating its cable television subscriber numbers in press releases and earnings reports.[12] The company has approximately 5.8 million subscribers and may have inflated its customer base by as much as 7 to 10 percent. Investigators also report that Adelphia kept two sets of books, one to show Wall Street and a second set with the correct information. The set of books for Wall Street contained much higher expenditures for capital improvements to upgrade its cable network than the company actually made.

Questions

a. What might a company expect to gain by inflating such numbers?
b. If a company were seeking a loan, what might be the impact of even a small falsification of numbers?
c. What are the implications of a company falsifying only its press releases in this matter, but not its earnings reports? Should the SEC take interest in this? Is falsifying its earnings reports more serious than falsifying its press releases?

Case 5.8
Reporting Extraordinary Items

Lang Hardware Company reports an extraordinary loss as an extraordinary item in its financial statements to emphasize the nonrecurring and unusual circumstances of the loss. In the same year the company wins a $10 million lawsuit, and the controller asks accountant Susan Powell to include the settlement as ordinary income in order to increase operating income.

Questions

a. What is the accounting issue involved in this situation? Does the controller's request meet GAAP standards?
b. What is the ethical dilemma?
c. Who is harmed by the differing treatment of extraordinary gains and losses? Who benefits?
d. What alternatives are available to Susan?
e. What would you do? Explain your decision to the controller.

Case 5.9
Loan Application

Marvin Construction is a small construction company specializing in residential remodeling projects. The company has experienced a surge in business in the past year, due to improved economic conditions in the area. They have applied to the bank for a major expansion loan to purchase equipment that is needed for the company to double in size. The loan officer at the bank has requested financial statements for Marvin Construction before approving the loan. Marvin Smith, the owner of the business, has suggested that the accountant, Jim Pierson, provide the bank with a copy of the balance sheet, but not the income statement. Last year the company lost money due to unusually high expenses, so Marvin is afraid that the bank will deny the loan if they see the income statement. Jim does not think it honest to provide the bank with only a balance sheet when they have requested financial statements, but he does not want to ignore the request from the president.

Questions

a.   What is the ethical dilemma described in this problem?
b.   Identify several alternatives available to Jim.
c.   How do the accounting rules you have learned help you to address Jim's problem?
d.   Identify the interested parties involved in this decision. Who benefits? Who is harmed?
e.   What would you do? Why?

Case 5.10
Certifying Reports to the SEC

As controller for Anderson Manufacturing, Peter Ford is preparing the quarterly financial statements to be sent to the Securities and Exchange Commission. These reports must be filed with the regulatory agency by noon tomorrow. Susan Teo, company president, needs a copy of the statements so she can review them before signing off on the accuracy of the statements. Peter has been very busy setting up the accounts for a new division in the company and has not had time to prepare the quarterly reports. He knows that there is an error in the revenue accounts that needs to be adjusted but does not have time to calculate the correct amount before the noon deadline. He is not concerned about the error because the revenue account can be adjusted during the fourth quarter before the auditors arrive. He decides to submit the third-quarter reports with the error and correct the mistake in the fourth quarter. He believes that the president will not complain about the error as long as the company looks good. This should also make the analysts happy, since the quarterly earnings per share numbers will meet analyst's forecasts.

Questions

a.   What is the ethical dilemma discussed in this problem?
b.   Identify several alternatives available to Peter.
c.   Comment on Peter's belief that the president will not complain as long as the company looks good.
d.   Should Peter tell Susan about the error?
e.   How will Susan determine whether the financial statements are accurate before she signs them?
f.   What would you do? Explain your answer.

Case 5.11
Reporting Sales Returns

The Fresh Foods Grocery Store specializes in selling fresh vegetables and fruits, fresh meat, and other grocery items. Jennifer Smithson, controller, and Andrew Loebeck, financial accountant, are reviewing the current month's financial statements. Andrew has received a request from the purchasing department asking the accounting department to discontinue the practice of using a sales returns and allowances account in the income statement because it makes the statement difficult to understand. The purchasing manager does not see any reason to keep sales returns separate from sales, since the year-end financial statements list only net sales.

Questions

a.   What is the accounting issue discussed in this problem? Does the purchasing manager receive any useful information from the sales returns and allowances account?

b.   What interested parties would be harmed by this request? What parties would benefit?

c.   What is the ethical dilemma described in this situation?

d.   What decision would you make regarding the request from the purchasing department?

e.   Explain your decision to the manager of the purchasing department in language that a non-accountant would understand.

Case 5.12
Valuing Goodwill

Josh Scott and Lisa Marconi are reviewing the 2003 financial statements for Jones Manufacturing. Sales in the computer division have declined in the past year due to the economy and unfavorable exchange rates with their foreign customers. Since the computer division was purchased from a competitor three years ago, Josh knows that they will have to review the fair value of the division to determine if goodwill recorded at the time of the purchase should remain on the books. The financial vice president, Jason Bruce, suggests leaving the goodwill on the books until the following year, due to earnings pressure from outside stock market analysts. Jason knows that the president wants to meet the analysts' forecast for earnings of $.30 per share, and writing off the goodwill will make this impossible. He suspects, however, that the fair value of the division has declined from the original purchase price and that the goodwill is worthless.

Questions

a.   What recommendation should Josh and Lisa make to the financial vice president regarding the write-down of the asset?

b. Do GAAP rules tell you how to account for goodwill? Can you use the rules to resolve this dilemma?

c. If GAAP rules do not tell you how to make this decision, how will you decide the appropriate action to take regarding accounting for goodwill in the computer division? If the rules do not tell you how to resolve this dilemma, is there any principle underlying the accounting rules that might help?

PRO FORMA REPORTS AND PRESS RELEASES

Case 5.13
3Com Corporation, Pro-Forma Reporting

3Com Corporation reported a $12.8 million pro forma profit in its fourth-quarter earnings release.[13] Seven million dollars of the profit was an accounting gain that came from the sales of inventory that 3Com had written off as obsolete. In an earlier quarter, 3Com took a charge to write down the value of the inventory and then recognized a large profit, more than half the quarterly income, when the inventory was sold. The $7 million gain was not mentioned in the earnings release but was disclosed in a conference call with analysts.

In contrast to this treatment, the previous year 3Com had taken more than $300 million in inventory write-downs that it excluded from pro forma earnings. The company referred to the write-downs as "nonrecurring," indicating to investors that the write-downs should be ignored in evaluating company performance.

Questions

a. Are nonrecurring adjustments reported in earnings releases more likely to be gains or losses? Explain why?
b. Identify the interested parties. Who benefits? Who is harmed?
c. Assume your job in the company is to prepare the quarterly earnings releases. Will you use pro forma earnings in your disclosure? Explain to your boss the reason for your decision.
d. Evaluate the quality of information available to outside users of the financial statements. Was the information relevant and reliable? Did it present an unbiased assessment of the financial position of the firm?

Case 5.14
Pro Forma Earnings

The growing use of pro forma earnings was a cause of concern to accounting regulators. In December 2001, the SEC issued a formal warning to corporations that they could face lawsuits for issuing misleading pro forma financial information in their news releases, unless they fully explain how the numbers were calculated. Because there are no standards for pro forma earnings, companies have taken great liberties in disclosing earnings in their news releases. In news releases, pro forma earnings are disclosed under a variety of names: "recurring earnings," "operating earnings," and "earnings, excluding special items." These releases are usually intended to represent the company's financial situation in the most favorable light. Pro forma earnings typically are higher than accounting earnings because they often exclude significant business expenses, such as restructuring charges, merger-related expenses, unusual charges, goodwill amortization, and goodwill write-offs, and include all gains, such as gains from asset sales. Wall Street analysts have accepted pro forma earnings with little scrutiny regarding the validity of the earnings and have used the information in their stock research analysis.

Questions

a.   Why do companies use pro forma earnings instead of accounting earnings in their news releases?

b.   Why did the SEC issue the warning to corporations regarding their use of pro forma earnings? Even assuming that earnings reports do not include such disclosures, why would the SEC direct companies to explain the information in the companies' own news releases?

c.   Consider the case of a company writing off several billion dollars of goodwill because the fair value of the reporting entity has declined. How might pro forma earnings be used in a news release to make the company look better? Is this a valid use of pro-forma earnings? From an accountant's perspective, are there valid uses of pro forma earnings?

d.   Does the ordinary reader of the company news release understand the terms "operating income," and "earnings, excluding special items"? Do you think the reader realizes that these two earnings terms are not accounting income? What difference might this make? Is it reasonable to expect that readers might make good use of information released in this manner? Discuss your answers.

e.   Does the ordinary reader of the company news release understand the lack of conformity in defining pro forma earnings? If such a reader does not notice the lack of conformity, why is this a problem? (Who might be harmed? Who might benefit from this lack of understanding?)

f.   Does the use of pro forma earnings improve the quality of information available to outsiders? Does it make a difference that news releases may be more frequent than earnings reports or more accessible to large numbers of readers than the annual report of the company? Explain your view.

Case 5.15
Pro Forma Earnings Reports for eToys

eToys, an Internet toy retailer, in business from 1999–2001, used pro forma earnings in its news releases. For example, a *Los Angeles Times* press release relating to the second quarter of 1999 reported, "excluding nonrecurring items, eToys lost $32.1 million or –$.27 per share for the quarter. That was significantly better than the –$.28 a share loss predicted by analysts."[14] The second-quarter loss reported to the SEC was $44.9 million or –$.38 per share.[15]

Questions

a. Is it appropriate for the company to say that they met analysts' forecasts? Explain your answer.
b. Do you believe readers of the press release understood the information in the press release?
c. Should the company have released the SEC numbers in the same press release as the pro forma numbers?
d. Identify the interested parties that benefit from the company's use of pro forma earnings. Which parties are harmed?
e. Do you support the use of pro forma earnings in news releases? Why?
f. Does the use of pro forma earnings improve the quality of information available to outsiders? Explain your answer.

Case 5.16
Issuing Stock Dividends

Warren Westman prepares the press release for Sun Marketing covering the fourth-quarter dividend payment. The company paid a quarterly dividend for the past ten years, but this quarter it decided to issue a stock dividend rather than a cash dividend. This action preserves cash for a major expansion. Susan Sorenson, president of the company, advises Warren to report the positive aspects of this stock dividend; "Make it appear that the stockholders will benefit by this dividend and that it is as good for them as receiving a cash payment." Warren worries about the exact wording of the press release, because he does not believe the stockholders will buy his story.

Questions

a. What is the ethical dilemma described in this problem?
b. Is the ethical dilemma dependent on whether the stock dividend is a large stock dividend or a small stock dividend? Explain your answer.
c. Identify the interested parties who might be influenced by the wording of the press release. Who benefits by the rosy picture presented by Warren? Who is harmed? Must press releases faithfully represent the economic situation of the company?
d. What would you do if the stock dividend was a small stock dividend? Draft a brief press release to present this information in a responsible manner.
e. What would you do if the stock dividend was a large stock dividend? Draft a brief press release to present this information so outside readers will be knowledgeable about the dividend issue.

Case 5.17
Company Press Releases

Mary Larson, the director of public relations for St. John's Hospital, is preparing a news release related to the yearly audit. Mary notes that net income has increased by 20 percent and wants to highlight this increase as a measure of the hospital's success in controlling costs. Daren Anderson, the controller, knows that the increase in net income is related to a company decision to reduce the bad debt estimate and is unrelated to cost-control measures. Daren explains the increase to Mary, but she replies: "Readers of the news release will not take the time to review the annual report, so we can tell them that earnings have increased due to efficiency measures on our part and they will think we are trying to save them money. It is more interesting to say that our earnings have increased due to cost-control measures, rather than to say that we changed our method of estimating bad debts to generate the increase. Besides, it's my job to make the hospital look good."

Questions

a.   What is the ethical dilemma in this situation?
b.   Based on your knowledge of GAAP, what is the correct answer to this dilemma? According to GAAP, must the information of press releases match the information disclosed in the annual report?
c.   What interested parties will be affected by the media release?
d.   Give your opinion on the following statement, citing reasons for your opinion: "Because Mary Larson, the director of public relations, is most directly responsible for the media release, Daren Anderson has no real responsibility in this matter."
e.   What would you do?

FOOTNOTE AND SUPPLEMENTAL DISCLOSURES

Case 5.18
Contingent Liabilities for Environmental Pollution

John Anderson, the controller for TLC Construction Company, is preparing the financial statements for the current year. Several lawsuits have been filed against the company for their role in applying a waterproofing compound, Globby 700, in the Clay County Courthouse. The waterproofing compound is designed to be applied at 1/16th of an inch. The lawsuits allege that TLC Construction Company was negligent by applying this compound as much as 1 inch thick. Many courthouse employees have been driven from the building due to the toxic fumes emitted by the chemicals. Employees at the courthouse have complained of a variety of physical symptoms, including bronchitis, burning throats, night sweats, and tingling fingers, plus general symptoms of nausea. Many offices have moved out of the courthouse and are seeking to recover damages from the company for the inconvenience and physical symptoms reported. The attorney for TLC Construction is concerned about the claims and will vigorously defend them in a court of law. The president of the company, Sara Adams, would like Anderson to ignore the contingent liability issue presented by the lawsuits because the company is not in very good shape this year. He hesitates to follow her orders because his sister works at the courthouse, and he knows that she has been very ill. It appears to Anderson that the claims made in the lawsuit may be valid. He believes that a contingent liability for at least $50 million should be recorded to cover the costs of cleaning up this "sick" building.

Questions

a. What is the ethical dilemma discussed in this situation?
b. Identify the interested parties affected by this decision. Who benefits? Who is harmed?
c. What are Anderson's alternatives? Do the alternatives express bias toward a predetermined result?
d. Based on your knowledge of GAAP, would you be able to resolve this dilemma? What would you do? Why?

Case 5.19
Contingent Liabilities

John Flynn, the controller for Wilson Construction Company, is preparing the financial statements for the current year. Several lawsuits have been filed against the company for its role in constructing an office building that collapsed. The president of the company, Harold Wilson, wants to ignore the potential liability. John believes that the loss is probable and the liability should be estimated, even though the lawsuits will take several years to settle. He would like to record a long-term contingent liability of $20,000,000.

Harold argues, "Because we can delay recording the liability if we say that no estimate is possible, we should avoid recording any liability this year. Let's just footnote the potential liability and see how the lawsuits develop. Besides, I can't go to the bank to obtain an operating loan for next year with that size of liability on my books!"

Questions

a.   What is the ethical dilemma described in this problem?
b.   Based on your knowledge of GAAP, what should the company do?
c.   Identify the interested parties affected by the decision to delay the recording of the liability. Who benefits? Who is harmed?
d.   What would you do? Why?
e.   Assume you believe the liability should be recorded this year. How would you explain your decision to the company president?

Case 5.20
Recording Trading Securities

Accountant Ron Simmons wants to disclose the cost of certain trading securities in the investment account in the footnotes. His supervisor, concerned about the decline in market value compared to the cost of these securities, does not want to call attention to this decline. The supervisor instructs Simmons to put the market value on the balance sheet and to avoid disclosing the cost in the footnote.

Questions

a.   What ethical issue is posed by the choice between these forms of disclosure?
b.   Are the interests of different parties in the company's method of disclosure? Which stakeholders benefit? Which stakeholders are harmed?
c.   What would you do?

Case 5.21
Annual Report Disclosures

In the supplementary information of its annual report, Scheel's Hardware, Inc., declares that its earnings have increased by 10 percent, using an earnings number that includes unusual, nonrecurring gains. The actual increase for operating income is only 2 percent. The income statement for Scheel's Hardware has correctly reported ordinary income and extraordinary items. The auditor is reviewing the supplemental information and is puzzled by this discrepancy. She has asked Bruce Dahlberg, the controller of Scheel's, to explain the difference.

Questions

a. What is the accounting issue involved in this method of reporting earnings increases in the supplemental disclosure section of the annual report? Do GAAP standards help you respond to this ethical dilemma?
b. Who are the interested parties in this situation? Who benefits? Who is harmed?
c. What should Bruce do?

Case 5.22
Annual Report Disclosures

Accountant Kari Hurd's supervisor asks her to include in the supplemental information of the annual report some comments on the dedicated and hard-working workforce that distinguishes Corwin Motors from its competitors. Kari knows that such remarks cannot be supported objectively in the financial statements. She is unsure whether to comply with this request. It doesn't seem right, but she can't think of any reason not to include this information.

Questions

a. What should Kari do? Advertisers frequently make such claims. Can you think of any reason why she should not comply with this request?
b. Who are the interested parties in this situation? Who benefits? Who is harmed?
c. Will this material mislead the interested parties?
d. What would you do if your supervisor asked you to comply with this request? Why?

Case 5.23
Reviewing the Management Discussion and Analysis Section of the Annual Report

Computer Systems, Inc., has had three good years in marketing its personal computers and software packages for office use. During this period, the profit margin on sales has increased 20 percent annually. Earnings per share have increased 10 percent annually and the price earnings ratio has grown steadily. Sarah Todd, the financial vice president, and Lance Thorn, the controller, are preparing the year-end financial statements and the accompanying management discussion that projects the company's performance. During this time, Sarah and Lance hear a pessimistic market analysis for office PCs, which argues that the market has been saturated during the previous six months. Sarah wants the management discussion to emphasize the trend of increased sales and to project it into the future. Lance is more cautious and does not think it reasonable in this instance to assume that past performance is a good predictor of future sales.

Questions

a. Is there an ethical dilemma in Sarah and Lance's disagreement? Explain.
b. Normally, a critical assumption of financial statement analysis is that the past is a reasonable prediction for the future. When might this assumption be set aside or qualified?
c. Based on your knowledge of GAAP, can this ethical dilemma be resolved? What do GAAP rules say about the management discussion section of financial statements?
d. Should the management discussion section reflect Sarah and Lance's knowledge of the market analysis; that is, should it show their differing views to the readers?
e. What would you do? Explain your decision.

Case 5.24
Recording Contingent Liabilities

The Environmental Protection Agency has notified Tennant Corporation that it will be assessed a portion of the cleanup cost for the Inver Grove Heights Toxic Waste Disposal Site. Tennant Corporation used this disposal site in the 1960s to dispose of its toxic waste. The estimated cost of clean up is $40,000,000 and Tennant Corporation will be assessed 10 percent of the cleanup cost based on its use of the facility. The cleanup will take eight years and is scheduled to begin next year in 2004. Tennant Corporation will be required to pay $500,000 per year for the next eight years. Eleanor Anderson and Steve Frank, accountants for Tennant Corporation, are trying to determine how to record this potential liability. They are almost finished with the 2003 financial statements, and they are not excited about adding either a $4,000,000 expense or a $500,000 expense to the income statement. Eleanor suggests footnote disclosure at most and would prefer to ignore the liability. Steve believes that the entire expense and liability should be recorded in 2003, since the notice has been received from the Environmental Protection Agency.

Questions

a. What is the appropriate method of reporting this expense, according to GAAP standards?
b. What is the ethical issue presented in this problem?
c. Who is harmed by nondisclosure? Who benefits?
d. What would you do? Explain your answer to your boss, the controller of Tennant Corporation.

Endnotes

[1] "A chronology of Enron's woes," *The Wall Street Journal,* October 3, 2002.

[2] "The fall of Enron," *Business Week Online,* December 17, 2001.

[3] Mitchell Pacelle, "Enron report gives details of deals that masked debt," *The Wall Street Journal,* September 23, 2002.

[4] Jathon Sapsford and Paul Beckett, "Citigroup deals helped Enron to disguise its debts as trades," *The Wall Street Journal,* July 22, 2002.

[5] Anne Maire Squeo, "Raytheon is said to be in talks to settle SEC disclosure charges," *The Wall Street Journal,* July 17, 2002.

[6] Vanessa O' Connell, "Interpublic restates results due and improper accounting," *The Wall Street Journal,* August 14, 2002.

[7] Rachel Emma Silverman, "GE's annual report bulges with data in bid and address post-error concerns," *The Wall Street Journal*, March 11, 2002.

[8] Ibid.

[9] Richards, Bill, and Thurm, Scott, "Boston Chicken Cases Mirrors Enron Failure," *The Wall Street Journal,* March 13, 2002.

[10] U.S. Securities and Exchange Commission, "SEC Charges Adelphia and Rigas Family with Massive Financial Fraud," http://www.sec.gov/mews/press/2002-110.

[11] Ibid.

[12] Ibid.

[13] Robin Sidel, "3Com inventory gain basis faults of pro-forma results," *The Wall Street Journal*, July 19, 2002.

[14] Karen, Kaplan, "eToys posts huge gain in sales, along with big loss: In its first quarter as a public company, online retailer sells $8 million of merchandise and loses $20.8 million," *The Los Angeles Times,* July 28, 1999.

[15] 8-K report SEC, www.sec.gov, July 1999.

Chapter 6
Management Fraud and Accounting Choice

[handwritten marginalia: SEC: What audit failures result in SEC action against auditor?]

[handwritten marginalia: M. Essayed, measure rate of choice, v. fraud/no-fraud or v. restate/no-restate]

This chapter focuses on fraud, the deliberate misrepresentation of the economic situation, and the accounting choices that are intended to misstate financial information. Companies sometimes choose not to follow generally accepting accounting principles (GAAP) in their efforts to mislead outsiders. The companies may have a number of motivations for their actions: to falsify company performance prior to mergers or the securing of loans, to mislead Wall Street analysts so that stock prices will not decline, to meet the conditions for management to receive reward incentives, or to deceive outside investors. While some accounting choices may not be fraudulent, they may not be consistent with accounting concepts and principles, such as reliability or relevance, and these choices do not clearly and accurately express the economic situation of the transactions.

Problems related to management fraud and accounting choice are presented in three categories: (1) earnings restatements; (2) management fraud; and (3) accounting choice.

EARNINGS RESTATEMENTS

Case 6.1
Hanover Compressor, Earnings Restatement

In February 2002, Hanover Compressor restated its results for 2000 and 2001 because of improper accounting for an off-balance sheet partnership.[1] Financial information concerning the adjustments follows (all numbers in millions).

Year	Net Income Originally Reported	Net Income after First Restatement in February 2002	Net Income after Second Restatement in March 2002	Net Income after Third Restatement in August 2002
2000	$58.7	$51.2		$49.7
2001	$64.5	$63.1	$60.9	

The 2001 financial numbers report net income for the first nine months of the year.[2] The settlements are small as a percentage of net income, but the stock price did not react well to the adjustments, closing at $7.62 on August 5, 2002, from a 52-week high of $32.50.

Hanover has blamed the bookkeeping problems on poor internal controls and has said it will do better in the future. Two top executives and the chief financial officer resigned when the restatements were announced.[3] The SEC is investigating whether Hanover improperly booked revenue and profit from an off-balance sheet partnership to inflate revenue at a time when the company executives and the company sold million of shares of stock and the company sold convertible debt.[4]

Questions

a. Why is the SEC concerned about revenue misstatements when company executives sell stock or issue debts? Consider issues of timeliness, neutrality, and faithful representation.
b. Identify the interested parties in the transaction. Who benefits? Who is harmed?
c. Is it likely that the errors were caused by poor internal controls or by management decisions at the top? What are the implications of either answer?

Case 6.2
Rent-Way, Expense Understatement

Rent-Way, the nation's second-largest company of rent-to-own stores, estimated that its expenses had been improperly misstated by $25 to $35 million. The stock price dropped 72 percent to $6.50 in response to this announcement.[5] Two months later, the company raised its estimate of the misstatement to $55 to $65 million, and six months later the estimate of misstatement was more than doubled to about $127 million over a two-year period.

William Morgenstern started Rent-Way in 1981, after spending several years working as a manager in a rent-to-own store. In 1993, Morgenstern and Jeffrey Conway succeeded in making Rent-Way a public company. By 2001, Rent-Way had expanded to more than 1,000 stores. Revenue in fiscal 2000 was $595 million compared to $8.4 million in 1993. Rent-Way serves lower-income customers who rent televisions and furniture on a weekly basis.

When Matthew Marini, the controller, went on vacation, the company's new chief financial officer, William McDonnell, became suspicious about the high level of inventory in the stores. He discovered that Rent-Way's in-store inventory listing reported less inventory in the stores than had been reported on the corporate books. As he questioned the reports, employees came forward with information on the altered financial entries made under the direction of Marini. When asked by Morgenstern about the accounting improprieties, Marini talked about the pressure to meet analysts' earnings expectations. Marini was fired for the accounting manipulations. His boss, Jeffrey Conway, then the company's president and chief operating officer, was also asked to resign for his failure to supervise Marini in a proper fashion. William Morgenstern, the

102

chief executive officer of the company, led the charge to uncover the improprieties. Investigations found no evidence that he had knowledge of the accounting manipulation.

According to the report regarding the accounting irregularities, Marini manipulated expenses by recording some big expenses, such as vehicle maintenance, as capital expenditures, whose value could be written down over time rather than immediately. Several weeks before year-end, the company stopped recording accounts payable to reduce expenses. Marini also kept scrap furniture on the books as inventory, rather than writing off the asset, and he also limited the amount of missing and discarded inventory that could be written off by instructing managers to delay the write-offs until the next fiscal year.

For fiscal 1999, Marini's expense manipulation totaled $28 million, allowing the company to report operating income of $30.3 million rather than about $2.3 million. In 2000, the reduction of expense totaled $99 million.

Questions

a.   Identify the interested parties involved in the earnings manipulation. Who benefits? Who is harmed?
b.   Why might the controller feel compelled to increase net income to meet analysts' forecasts? Why might he care about this?
c.   Did the company act appropriately when the earnings manipulations were discovered? Should they have done something else? Something more? Give reasons for your answer.
d.   In a conversation with the CEO, Marini asked if he could keep his job. Do you think he understood the seriousness of his actions for the company? Did he violate accounting principles? Did he commit fraud?
e.   Were internal controls effective in this company? Explain your answer.

Case 6.3
Rite Aid, Earnings Restatements

The SEC filed accounting fraud charges in June 2002 against three former executives of Rite Aid Corporation.[6] The complaint alleges that Rite Aid, a drug store chain operating 3,500 stores, overstated its income every quarter from May 1997 to May 1999. The total misstatement was $1.6 billion, the largest restatement ever recorded. According to an SEC spokesman, "The charges announced today reveal a disturbing picture of dishonesty and misconduct at the highest level of a major corporation. Rite Aid's former senior management employed an extensive bag of tricks to manipulate the company's reported earning and defraud its investors."[7]

Martin Grass, Rite Aid's former chief executive and chairman, faces 36 charges ranging from accounting fraud to failure to disclose related party transactions and fabricating board minutes to obtain a bank line of credit to keep the company operating. Grass, the son of the company founder, inflated earnings to receive bonuses and other stock awards tied to financial performance. Rite-Aid's stock price fell to $2.69 per share in June 2002, a decline of almost 95 percent from its value of $50 per share in early 1999, when *The Wall Street Journal* first reported on the related-party transactions with the Grass family.

According to the complaint, executives recorded fictitious credits from vendors for damaged and outdated goods, falsified expense records, manipulated the accounts payable entries, took credits for drugs that customers didn't pick up, reversed entries for expenses that had already been paid, reduced cost of goods sold and accounts payable, and failed to account fully for inventory shrinkage. According to the complaint, business executives gave cash and the offer of a car to subordinates who covered the fictitious transactions. One of the fired executives received $6 million in company funds when he threatened to blow the whistle on the fraudulent activity.

RiteAid's auditor, KPMG, quit in 1999 and withdrew its opinions for 1997–1999. The government said the business executives lied extensively to KPMG. The SEC indictment alleges that Grass tried to defraud RiteAid even after he resigned from the company by creating letters authorizing severance pay to the top three executives and backdating the letters to a time when he was CEO.

Questions

a. Identify the interested parties in the management fraud at RiteAid. Who benefits from the fictitious accounting schemes? Who is harmed?
b. Clearly internal controls at the firm were not effective in preventing this fraud. What limitation of control systems makes this kind of inappropriate accounting activity difficult to detect?
c. Fraud charges were not filed against KPMG. Why might have company executives alone, rather than the auditor, been blamed for this illegal accounting scheme?

MANAGEMENT FRAUD

Case 6.4
Sonali, Requests for Financing

Surya P. "Pat" Patangay, a small gold-jewelry seller in Oceanside, California, easily defrauded Wells Fargo & Co. out of $14.5 million.[8] Patangay says his ruse worked because of lax standards at Ernst & Young. To obtain loans, he fabricated documents showing sales revenue of $70 million per year, but yearly sales never totaled more than $1.5 million. The auditors relied on copies of documents rather than originals, sent confirmations to 50 post office boxes of bogus customers, and, during an inventory count, failed to uncover fake gold.

In the mid-1980s, Patangay founded Sonali Corporation, a company importing ornate 22-karat gold, a purer gold than that usually sold in the United States. He sold the gold to American jewelers. Because jewelers did not pay for the gold until it was sold, and the foreign gold suppliers required cash on delivery of the gold, Patangay arranged financing with U.S. banks to cover the gold purchase. The financing from a bank covered the delay between his payments to suppliers and the jewelers' payments.

He approached the Bank of America for a small-business loan. The bank asked for financial records. Patangay had no financial records, so he created them in his office, starting with original documents and making fictitious documents using a copy machine. (For example, he took a receipt for a $10,000 sale and changed it to a $100,000 transaction.) Using this deception, he received an unsecured loan for $250,000.

Such techniques enabled Patangay to deceive auditors during their on-site visits. He reports that he showed Ernst & Young auditors "some real documents, nothing important. The receivables, payables, invoices, my bank statements, I made them up."[9] His bank statement scam, for example, created an illusion that millions of dollars were flowing through his company bank account. This involved altering original statements in a manner that should have been detected by the auditors. These "client-prepared documents" successfully fooled Ernst & Young. In this and other aspects of the audit, the accountants "never insisted on originals. If they had, I would have failed the audit."

In another matter, auditors did not notice the bogus list of 50 customers who supposedly owed money to the company because auditors failed to be alerted when the accounts receivable listing did not include street addresses. These letters were forwarded to 50 post office addresses Patangay himself rented, thus enabling him to pose as those customers and falsify confirmation responses.

When auditors examined gold and jewelry in Sonali's vault and safe-deposit boxes, the stock included lengthy spools of gold-plated costume chain. The auditors asked to take a sample chain for valuing, but Patangay suggested that they be satisfied with a pre-cut piece (of genuine gold that he had prepared) rather than cut the chain. The auditors complied with his request. Patangay, now facing legal punishment, does not blame the auditors for his troubles: "But their audit procedures have big flaws that people can take advantage of."[10]

Questions

a. What are some of the big flaws that Patangay exploited in his dealing with auditors?
b. What should auditors have done in their examination of Patangay's sales transaction documents? The bank statement materials?
c. What inventory procedure might have alerted the auditors to fraud?
d. Did Patangay's fabricating documents to secure bank loans serve any legitimate purpose? Assume that he got a loan from the Bank of America and was later able to repay it. Would any harm have been done? Explain your answer.
e. Identify the interested parties in this situation. Who was harmed? Who benefited?
f. Evaluate the quality of information presented to outsiders. Did the financial statements present the underlying economic reality of the transactions?

Case 6.5
Recording Revenue Transactions

Leslie Fay Companies reported widespread fraud at the company. According to a board audit committee report, the company engaged in several questionable business practices designed to increase net income. The following examples illustrate the accounting practices used by the company to increase sales revenue.

1. When sales fell below the budgeted numbers, the company "shipped" goods to trailers near one of their facilities, and reported sales for these transactions.
2. Company officials created fake sales by using corporate loans.
3. The company reported the gain from the sale of a division as operating income.
4. The company invoiced goods the final day of the quarter, even though the goods were not shipped until the next quarter.
5. The accounting department delayed the write-off of company loans even though it was apparent that Leslie Fay would not be repaid for the loans.

Questions

a. Identify the ethical dilemmas posed by the accounting practices described in items 1–5.
b. Members of the audit committee stated that it would have been difficult for management not to have known about the extensive inventory and sales fraud. Based on your knowledge of accounting principles, how would management discover each of the five "errors" discussed above?

Case 6.6
Recording Contingent Rental Fees

Wilson's Jewelry rents space in the West Acres Mall. The store is charged a rental fee of $8,000 per month, plus 7 percent of yearly profits over a base level of $3,000,000. The owner of the store, Jim Wilson, would like to keep net income under $3,000,000 to avoid paying the additional 7 percent. Jim tells the accountant David Andreason to increase warranty expense and bad debt expense to the point where net income is approximately $2,860,000.

Questions

a. What is the ethical dilemma described in this problem?
b. Identify the interested parties affected by the decision to increase the estimates of two expenses to keep net income below a certain point. Who benefits from this change? Who is harmed?
c. Why are estimates subject to this type of adjustment? Can the accountant prepare estimates in a responsible, ethical fashion?
d. Identify several alternatives available to David.
e. What would you do? Explain your answer.
f. Assume you decided not to follow the owner's directive. How would you explain your decision to Jim?

Case 6.7
Cash Distributions for a Privately Held Company

ABC Manufacturing is a small, privately held company. Management owns 60 percent of the stock, while others that are not associated with running the company own 40 percent. The company has been manufacturing components for luxury cars, but because of changing technology its equipment is obsolete. The managers are concerned about the ability of the company to survive. They have invested money and time in the company, and their ownership in the company is about to become worthless since they cannot modernize because of the cost. Barb Oliver, the president of the company, has a suggestion for the management group, "We currently have about $7 million of cash available. Let's use this cash to purchase our shares of stock as treasury stock. If we do this, when the value of the company drops and it files for bankruptcy, we will have taken as much cash out of the company as we can. This seems a fair way to reward the owners of the company for their hard work."

Questions

a. What is the ethical dilemma described in this problem?

b.   Why didn't the company president propose the alternative of a cash dividend of $7 million? This action would have the effect of distributing cash to the owners. (Hint: Which owners benefit?)

c.   Identify the interested parties affected by this decision. Who benefits by the purchase of treasury stock? Who is harmed?

d.   Does the company have any other alternatives available?

e.   What would you do? Explain your answer.

f.   If you were one of the creditors of this company affected by the bankruptcy, would you approve of their plan?

Case 6.8
Recognizing Revenue

John Lunde, the president of Gladden Manufacturing, is eligible for a bonus if net income increases by 15 percent. He has a simple plan designed to guarantee that he gets his bonus. He knows that Samuel Adams negotiated a large order on December 20, 2003. The goods will not be shipped until the middle of January, but since they are custom-manufactured and cannot be returned once they're ordered, he believes the revenue should be recognized in December. This will give him the revenue needed so that net income increases by 15 percent. Explaining the situation to the controller, Beth Duncan, he says, "The accounting rules require a company to recognize revenue when it has been earned. Surely we earned this revenue when we got the order. I want this revenue recognized in 2003, so I get my bonus. I have earned it and I do not want to lose it just because the goods were not shipped until 2004."

Questions

a.   What is the ethical dilemma described in this problem?

b.   According to accounting standards, how should revenue be recognized? Are there any situations where revenue is recognized based on an order? Based on your knowledge of GAAP, what should Beth do?

c.   If Beth is due for a yearly review and pay increase next month, should she try to please her boss so she gets a good raise?

d.   Identify the interested parties affected by this decision. Who benefits? Who is harmed?

e.   What would you do? Explain your decision.

Case 6.9
Internal Controls for Cash Disbursements

According to an article in a Midwestern newspaper, stealing $2.3 million from the Dakota Credit Union was simple. Joe Kramer, who lost the money gambling, was the

credit union's only full-time employee. Kramer said he began gambling to make the payments on a $50,000 loan to a friend, because the friend was unable to pay the loan. In a
one-year period, Kramer made 15 trips to Las Vegas, gambling to cover the $50,000 loan. Kramer, waiting for sentencing on a federal charge of looting, was fired from the credit union one week before the state Credit Union Board declared the institution insolvent and closed its doors.

Questions

a. In the absence of effective internal control, what factors might have influenced Kramer not to embezzle?
b. What internal controls might have prevented Kramer's theft?
c. Joe Kramer lives in a town with fewer than 500 people. Would you be suspicious, in a town of this size, if the manager of the credit union went to Las Vegas more than once a month? As a member of the credit union, what might you do to ensure that the manager was acting properly?

Case 6.10
Internal Controls in the Catholic Church

A recent article in *The Wall Street Journal* reported on several embezzlement cases in the Roman Catholic Church. According to the article, employees of the Catholic Church have stolen more than $3.5 million from the church in the last three years. Bishop Donald Trautman, who heads a church committee studying the thefts, was quoted: "There has been a breakdown in our whole society regarding honesty and the [commandment not to steal]. Unfortunately, we're part of that society and that culture." Some of the incidents reported in the article include the following:

1. John Weber, chief accountant of the Roman Catholic Diocese of Wilmington, Delaware, set fire to his computer and accounting records when he discovered he was to be sued for embezzling more than $1 million of diocese funds. Fellow employees had wondered how an accountant on a $40,000 per year salary could afford a $270,000 house, three or four cars, and a beach house. Weber told them he had inherited the money from his mother.
2. Reverend Martin Greenlaw was sued by the archdiocese in San Francisco for diverting $200,000 from church funds to purchase a house. The lawsuit alleges that Father Greenlaw diverted money from bingo games, bequests, wedding stipends, and Sunday collections while he served as pastor for two local churches.
3. Frederick C. Keppler, the comptroller of the Diocese of Burlington, Vermont, diverted into his personal accounts $212,187 from special fund drives for world relief organizations. Helping several churches to develop computer

systems, Keppler overcharged churches by $30,759 for the computers and software they received.

4. William J. McCook, the financial director for the archdiocese in Denver, was charged with embezzling $600,000. The lawsuit alleged that the money came from selling gravel taken out of the cemetery.

5. Molly Brusstar, the administrator of employee benefits for the Diocese of Arlington, Virginia, was charged with embezzling money by writing checks to sisters in the Order of Saint Clare to enroll the sisters in a local weight-loss program. The Order of Saint Clare is a cloistered, contemplative order, so this action appeared unreasonable to officials in the diocese. Ms. Brusstar also issued phony retirement checks to individuals she had created.[11]

Questions

a. What internal controls might have prevented each of these actions?
b. Do you believe there has been a breakdown in our society regarding honesty? Explain your answer.
c. Are not-for-profit organizations, like the Catholic Church, more susceptible to embezzlement than for-profit organizations? Why do you think this?

ACCOUNTING CHOICE

Case 6.11
Implementation of New FASB Standards

In September 2001, the Financial Accounting Standards Board issued FASB No. 142 entitled "Goodwill and Other Assets." This statement was effective for fiscal years beginning after December 15, 2001, with earlier implementation encouraged. Welle Construction Company is reviewing the requirements of this FASB to determine whether to implement this statement in their annual report dated December 31, 2001 or December 31, 2002. John Harrison, controller of Welle Construction, suggests implementing the new FASB in 2001. Angela Evans would rather delay until 2002. She says "The requirements of FASB 142 will have a significant impact on the financial statements for Welle Construction, and I would prefer to delay implementation as long as possible."

Questions

a. Based on your knowledge of GAAP, speculate on the impact this statement will have on the balance sheet and income statement.
b. Present an argument for early implementation.
c. Present an argument for delaying implementation until the latest date possible.
d. Would your decision change if the implementation of FASB No. 142 had a positive impact on net income?
e. How will you choose between these two alternatives?
f. What is the role of ethics in determining when you should implement new financial standards. To act ethically and provide outside users with the most complete set of financial disclosure possible, are you always required to choose early implementation?

Case 6.12
Cash Salary Payments

Chris's Barbecue and Grill employs 50 people in its restaurant. Forty employees are full-time and the rest are part-time. Chris hires an accountant to prepare the monthly financial statements and to write the payroll checks for the full-time employees, but he pays the part-time help in cash. The appropriate payroll deductions are made from the checks for the full-time employees, but the part-time employees are simply paid their hourly wage. By paying these employees in cash, Chris avoids matching their social security deductions and paying federal and state unemployment tax and workers' compensation on the employees. Chris believes that the employee like being paid in cash because they can choose whether or not to report this income on their income tax returns.

Questions

a. Is Chris's method of payment legal?
b. What is the ethical dilemma for the accountant hired by the restaurant? Do you believe the accountant is aware of the cash payments to the part-time employees?
c. The AICPA Code of Professional Conduct requires that client information be kept confidential. According to this rule, can the CPA report Chris's Barbecue and Grill to the tax authorities?
d. What are the advantages or disadvantages for Chris's Barbecue and Grill if the company hired an accountant not licensed as a CPA (such an accountant would not be bound by the accountant's code of conduct)?
e. Identify the parties affected by the decision to make cash payments to the part-time employees. Who benefits? Who is harmed?
f. What alternatives are available to the accountant?
g. What would you do? Explain your answer.

Case 6.13
Implementing Standards for Toxic Waste Disposal

New and more stringent federal standards for toxic waste disposal were mandated in 2005. Hughes Chemical Company has estimated that the new standards will cost $4,000,000 per year above the current cost. A panel of the company's scientists reports that the new standards are reasonable and important to ensure public safety in the future. The panel recommends that the company comply as soon as feasible. The controller, Donna Stevens, argues that Hughes should comply only with the letter of the law and should delay implementation of the new procedures until the 2005 deadline. The financial vice president, Tom Andrews, disagrees and argues that the company has a moral obligation to go beyond the letter of the law and to be socially responsible. He favors early implementation of the new toxic waste disposal procedures.

Questions

a. Identify the parties affected by this decision.
b. Outline two arguments: the first, supporting the controller's position to save money; the second, arguing for the vice president's view to "be socially responsible."
c. In your opinion, might two current stockholders disagree on the decision to implement the disposal procedures before the law required it?
d. Based on your knowledge of GAAP, select the best argument in part b.
e. What would you do? Explain your position to the board of directors of Hughes Chemical Company.

Case 6.14
Recording a Change in Accounting Principle

The Sunshine Food Company has decided to change its method of calculating depreciation expense from an accelerated method to straight-line. In revising the depreciation calculation, Andrew Klommer, the controller, discovered a math error on the depreciation schedule for last year. The total depreciation last year was $1,800,000. It was recorded as $2,800,000. The change in accounting principle decreases depreciation expense by $1,000,000. Andrew would like to make both of these changes at the same time by debiting accumulated depreciation by $1,000,000 and crediting income effect of change in accounting principle by $1,000,000. Because his bonus is calculated based on the increase in net income, he would like to run both of these changes through the income statement. He doesn't think anyone will catch this mistake, because management is expecting an increase in net income anyway due to the accounting principle change.

Questions

a. What is the correct accounting treatment for the changes made by Andrew?
b. What is the ethical dilemma described in this problem?
c. Based on your knowledge of GAAP, what should Andrew do?
d. Why is Andrew tempted not to follow GAAP standards? Would he also be tempted if his bonus were not connected to net income?
e. What would you do? Why?

Case 6.15
Implementing FASB No. 141

In September 2001, the Financial Accounting Standards Board issued FASB No. 141 entitled "Business Combinations." This statement was effective for all business combinations initiated after June 30, 2001. Anderson Windows is reviewing the requirements of this FASB to determine whether to implement this statement in their annual report dated December 31, 2001 or December 31, 2002. James Pearson, controller of Welle Construction, suggests recording the combination of assets purchased on October 1, 2001, as a pooling-of-interests since the business combination was initiated before June 30, 2001. Wendy Ivy would rather use the provisions of FASB No. 141 and record the combination of assets as a purchase.

Questions

a. Based on your knowledge of GAAP, speculate on the impact this statement will have on the balance sheet and income statement.
b. Present an argument for early implementation.
c. Present an argument for delaying implementation until the latest date possible.

d.   Would your decision change if the implementation of FASB No. 141 had a positive impact on net income?
e.   How will you choose between these two alternatives?
f.   What is the role of ethics in determining when you should implement new financial standards? To act ethically and provide outside users with the most complete set of financial disclosure possible, are you always required to choose early implementation?

Case 6.16
Recording Accounting Changes

Warner-Larson Company, a manufacturer of windows and doors, has a major loan due at the bank next year. The provisions of the loan specify that it can be renewed for another five years if the financial position of the firm justifies the five-year extension. The company wants the money available to expand and does not want to repay the loan next year. The president of the company, Alan Johnson, has suggested that the accountant, Susan Andrews, make several accounting changes designed to increase net income for the current year in order to assure that the bank will extend the time period on the loan. The company will probably change all these items back after the loan is generated, but for now the changes will assure that the payment schedule is extended. Alan suggests the following changes: (1) record revenue timely, but delay recording year-end expenses until the following year; (2) change the depreciation of its assets from three to seven years; and (3) ship several major customers extra inventory at year-end to increase sales revenue.

Questions

a.   Explain how each of these items will increase net income.
b.   What is the ethical dilemma described in this problem?
c.   Based on your knowledge of GAAP, are these changes appropriate?
d.   From an ethical point of view, should Susan Andrews comply with the president's request?

Case 6.17
Recording a Permanent Impairment in Asset Value

In 2003, Vision Manufacturing expanded production of CD players through the construction of a plant and custom-designed machinery costing $114,000,000. Within a year of the plant opening, the company lost 75 percent of its market to the competitor's CD players manufactured with MP3 components and was forced to reduce operations in the new plant. The board of directors of Vision Manufacturing asks advice from Eric Matthews, the financial vice president, on the disposition of the plant and equipment.

Matthews, optimistic about recapturing a portion of the market through minor technological improvements to the current CD players, maintains that no impairment in value has occurred. Sarah Rice, the controller, who has just purchased a CD player with MP3 capability from the competitor, thinks that the plant and equipment should be written down to market value and sold quickly.

Questions

a.   What is the ethical dilemma in this situation?
b.   Which parties are harmed by Matthew's suggestion? By Rice's position?
c.   What decision would you make? Why?
d.   Might footnote disclosure of potential impairment in value be used instead of either Matthews' or Rice's approach? If so, discuss the ethical implication of using footnote disclosure in this situation.

Case 6.18
Recording Research and Development costs

In 2003, Accounting Software, Inc., developed an instructional software package for teaching accounting to be used in introductory accounting classes in the university setting. This software cost $10,500,000 to develop and will sell for $35 per package. Although there are thousands of entry-level accounting students, this is a new market for the company.

Questions

a.   Prepare an argument to advocate expensing the development cost in the current year.
b.   Offer an argument for capitalizing the development cost over its estimated useful life.
c.   Identify the interested parties and tell how they are affected by each approach.
d.   What would you do?
e.   Which of the arguments in parts a and b above is currently favored by GAAP? How does GAAP help you answer this question? Explain your answer.

Case 6.19
Expensing Capital Expenditures

Collier College follows the policy of expensing all computers in the year of purchase, rather than depreciating them over their useful life. Tuition might be lower this year if the computers were depreciated over their useful life of three years. Is the practice of expensing the computers unethical behavior on the part of the college?

Questions

a. What is the ethical dilemma described in this problem?
b. Based on your knowledge of GAAP, are you able to answer this question?
c. What policy would you recommend to the college controller?

Case 6.20
Recording Frequent Flyer Promotions

Industry analysts estimate that airlines have sold more than 34.6 billion miles of free travel as promotions to hotels, phone companies, and car rental agencies, with an estimated cost of $2.3 billion if passengers use their ticket eligibility. The airlines have assumed that the free mileage would be used to fill seats that might not have been used without the promotional programs. George Smith, accountant for American Airways, notes the sizable increase in potential passengers who have earned frequent flyer miles from non-airline sources during the last 22 months. If these people choose to travel in the upcoming year, Smith believes that American Airways' costs might increase as it provides for the extra seating. Accordingly, Smith recommends deferring a portion of the revenue from all ticket sales to frequent flyer passengers and recording it as a long-term liability for future seating.

Questions

a. Does Smith's decision have an ethical dimension? If so, describe its features.
b. Identify the interested parties in this situation. Who benefits? Who is harmed?
c. Explain the GAAP rule on revenue recognition in this situation. Does your knowledge of GAAP help you resolve the ethical dilemma?
d. What would you do? Explain your decision.

Case 6.21
Preparing the Statement of Cash Flows

Current accounting standards permit accountants to prepare the statement of cash flows using either the direct or the indirect methods.

Questions

a. Describe the two methods that might be used to prepare the statement of cash flows.
b. Identify particular stakeholders who might benefit from the clarity provided by the statement of cash flows prepared according to the direct method in contrast to the indirect method.

c. If the statement of cash flows prepared according to the direct method presents the operating information more clearly, why do more than 95 percent of companies preparing this statement use the indirect method?

d. Are any parties harmed when the company uses the indirect method to prepare the statement of cash flows?

Case 6.22
Calculating Operating Cash for the Statement of Cash Flows

Montgomery Manufacturing applies for an expansion loan from the bank. After reviewing the company's balance sheet, income statement, and statement of cash flows, the loan officer tells the controller, Jason Stevenson, that he will not be able to approve the loan until the company can demonstrate a positive cash flow from operations on the statement of cash flows. Jason and his assistant, Mike Welker, discuss ways to generate a positive cash flow for the next quarter. Mike suggests that they make the following changes:

1. Increase the asset lives of the buildings and equipment to decrease depreciation expense.
2. Sell excess equipment at a loss to generate a positive cash flow.
3. Decrease the balance in accounts receivable by being more aggressive about collection efforts.
4. Delay paying the accounts payable for 45–60 days rather than the normal 30 at the end of the quarter.
5. Decrease the inventory balance to increase cash flows.

Jason is unsure whether these changes would work because he finds the statement of cash flows hard to understand. He wonders, "Even if they work, are they ethical?"

Questions

a. Determine the impact on the cash flows from operations of the five changes. Will they have the desired effect on the cash from operations?

b. What are the ethical dilemmas discussed in this case? Is it ethical to increase your cash flow from operations by making these changes?

c. Identify the parties affected by the changes suggested by Mike. Who benefits? Who is harmed?

d. What would you do? Explain your decision.

Case 6.23
Delaying Payments on Accounts Payable

A debt covenant for bonds issued by St. Andrews Hospital requires the company to report cash from operations of $1,000,000 at the end of each year of operations. The controller, Steve Savage, reviews the cash flow statement on December 1, 2003, to determine if the hospital will meet this covenant by December 31, 2003. Currently the cash flow statement shows a balance of $900,000 for the net cash provided by operations. Steve's supervisor, Julie Peterson, believes that he can increase this balance by year-end either by decreasing the accounts receivable balance or by increasing the accounts payable balance. Steve knows that it is impossible to decrease the accounts receivable balance by year-end. Most of the revenue comes from third-party insurance payments, and there is no way to convince the insurance companies to pay faster. The only way to increase the accounts payable balance by the necessary amount is to delay payment of the weekly bills for the last three weeks in December. This action will make creditors unhappy, but it is the easiest way to meet the debt covenant requirement.

Questions

a. Will taking Julie's suggestion have the desired result? Explain the accounting impact.
b. Does Steve face an ethical dilemma with Julie's suggestions for altering the statement of cash flows? Describe this dilemma.
c. Identify the interested parties affected by the decision to increase the accounts payable balance at year-end. Who benefits from this decision? Who is harmed?
d. Suggest other alternatives that might be available to Steve.
e. What would you do? Explain your answer.

Case 6.24
Evaluating Performance-Based Compensation Plans

K&B Department Store is considering a performance-based compensation plan for its executives, which links the bonus payments to increases in net income. The company currently uses LIFO inventory valuation and accelerated depreciation, and estimates warranty expense at 5 percent of net sales and bad debt expense at 7 percent of net sales.

Questions

a. If a performance-based compensation plan is adopted, what ethical dilemma might an accountant confront in the choice between LIFO and FIFO? Between accelerated and straight-line depreciation?
b. Under what conditions might an accountant be influenced to alter his or her estimate of warranty or bad debt expense?
c. State the features of the ethical dilemma posed by the presence of a

performance-based compensation plan. Think of interested parties and their interests, the accountant's own interests, and the specificity or ambiguity of GAAP.

d.   If performance-based compensation plans often cause ethical dilemmas, why are they used by companies?

Case 6.25
Recording Lease transactions

Smith Construction entered into a three-year lease agreement for fax machines for the corporate office. The lease agreement qualifies as an operating lease in all respects, except there is a bargain purchase option attached to the agreement. The bargain purchase option specifies that at the end of the three-year lease, Smith Construction can purchase the fax machines for $300 when the estimated market value is $450. The controller, Susan James, is preparing to record the leases as capital arrangements, even though she does not want to add the additional liability to the balance sheet. At lunch, Susan discusses this dilemma with Keith Olson, the chief financial officer. Keith says, "I don't know much about fax machines, but it seems like we should be able to get around this dilemma by arguing that the bargain purchase option is not really a bargain because fax technology will change so much in the three years. It's your decision, but give it some thought and see if you agree with me."

Questions

a.   Based on your knowledge of GAAP, what is the accounting issue in this situation? Why does Susan want to avoid recording the lease liability on the financial statements?
b.   What ethical issue is at stake in this situation?
c.   Identify the interested parties in this problem. Who benefits? Who is harmed?
d.   Should the controller's argument be accepted if he does not really know much about fax technology? Would it make a difference if the controller were knowledgeable about the pace of change of fax technology?
e.   What would you do? Explain your decision to your roommate who works as a commercial artist.

Case 6.26
Classifying Tax Loss Carryforwards

Dillingham Construction Company incurred a $10,000,000 net operating loss during 2003. The financial vice president of the company, Ann Fallon, wants to set up a deferred tax asset based on the entire net operating loss. She thinks that there are good prospects for a profitable year in 2004 or 2005 and that the deferred tax asset can be used to reduce tax liability in the future. The controller, Steve Thompson, is pessimistic and does not believe that the performance of the company can be quickly altered. He thinks there should be either no tax-deferred asset or an asset based on only half the amount, because this amount is a better estimate of the future prospects of the company.

Questions

a.   Based on your knowledge of GAAP, what do the accounting rules tell you about the appropriate treatment of the operating loss?
b.   What ethical dilemma is suggested by this disagreement? Does reliance on GAAP allow you to solve this dilemma? Why?
c.   Respond to the following statement: "No particular stakeholder will be harmed, regardless of the decision concerning the tax-deferred asset."
d.   What would do? Would you answer differently if you knew that the company had experienced three consecutive years of losses or if the 2003 loss was an isolated event? Why?

Case 6.27
Estimating a Liability

Ernie Mancini, the controller for Northstar Airlines, is reviewing the potential liability for the airline's frequent-flyer program. He notes that the 2004 estimate of the cost incurred to fly passengers under the program had been underestimated. The estimate was a 5 percent deferral of sales revenue, but the actual deferral was 10 percent. Citing an industry-wide analysis that a higher proportion of frequent flyers are using their ticket eligibility than previously, Mancini recommends a new estimate of at least 10 percent, matching the actual deferral of 2004. Financial vice president Cindy Evans does not think it is good practice to lower net income in this manner. She wants to retain the 5 percent estimate for 2005, even if the previous estimate was too low.

Questions

a.   What is the ethical dilemma that Ernie and Cindy face?
b.   Based on your knowledge of GAAP, can you resolve this dilemma?
c.   Identify the interested parties in this situation. Who benefits? Who is harmed?
d.   What alternatives are available to Ernie and Cindy?
e.   What would you do? Explain your answer in a manner that would make the reasons for your decision clear to your best friend.

Case 6.28
Calculating Accounting Estimates

Johnson Manufacturing plans to issue stock in 2004 to raise cash to build a new manufacturing facility. Susan Anderson, the controller for the company, is working on the 2003 financial statements. She has been told by the company president, Dave Johnson, that she will receive a large bonus if she can make net income as large as possible. Dave would like to present a favorable picture of the financial results in 2003 so that when the stock is issued in 2004, it will draw a good price. The company is ready to begin marketing its products nationally and needs the new facility to support the increased sales. Susan plans to make three changes in accounting estimates to increase net income: lengthen the asset lives for depreciation on the buildings (from twenty to thirty years) and on the equipment (from seven to ten years), and decrease the percentage of uncollectible accounts from 4 to 2 percent. The original estimates for the asset lives are still valid, but it will be easy to increase net income in this manner. These changes will make the company appear profitable in 2003, particularly compared to previous years. Changing accounting estimates seems like an easy way to increase net income.

Questions

a. Will the changes suggested by Susan increase net income? Explain how.
b. Does Susan face an ethical dilemma when she changes accounting estimates to increase net income? If so, describe the dilemma.
c. Based on your knowledge of GAAP, how might the changes proposed by Susan be legitimate? Do those conditions apply in this situation?
d. How would an independent auditor evaluate whether the changes were justified?
e. Identify the interested parties affected by Susan's decision to increase net income. Who benefits? Who is harmed?
f. Is Susan justified in making these changes because the accounting standards permit a great deal of flexibility in setting estimates?
g. What would you do? Why?

Endnotes

[1] Aaron Elstein, "Questioning the books: Hanover Compressor restates its results for second time," *The Wall Street Journal*, March 29, 2002.

[2] Aaron Elstein, "Hanover Compressor restates results for third time in 2002, *The Wall Street Journal,* August 5, 2002.

[3] Scott McCartney, "Two top executives resign from Hanover Compressor," *The Wall Street Journal*, August 5, 2002.

[4] Alexei Barrionuevo, "Hanover booked revenue in 2000, 2001 from project it knew would be delayed," *The Wall Street Journal*, March 11, 2002.

[5] Queena Sook Kim, "Rent-Way details improper bookkeeping," *The Wall Street Journal*, June 8, 2001.

[6] Scott Kilman, "Federal said jury charges executives in Rite Aid probe," *The Wall Street Journal*, June 24, 2002.

[7] U.S. Securities & Exchange Commission, "SEC Announces Fraud Charges against Former Rite Aid Senior Management," http://www.sec.gov/news/press/2002-92.htm., June 21, 2002.

[8] Jeff D. Opdyke, "Fraud perpetrator points finger at auditors for lax standards," *The Wall Street Journal,* March 1, 2002.

[9] Ibid.

[10] Ibid.

[11] John Fialka, "Unholy acts: church officials' thefts dismay Catholics," *The Wall Street Journal*, June 27, 1995, pp. B1–B2.

Chapter 7
Professional Conduct in Accounting

A variety of professional codes of conduct shape the professional behavior of accountants. The cases in this chapter indicate a number of violations of professional conduct by accountants or by auditors who fail in their oversight functions. A number of cases and questions are designed to test your knowledge of the specific codes of conduct and ability to apply their canons to "real life" circumstances. These professional codes include the *AICPA Code of Professional Conduct* and the requirements for independence established by the SEC. Particular emphasis is placed on audit situations and matters related to internal control.

Problems related to professional conduct in accounting are presented in three categories: (1) audit failures; (2) AICPA Professional Code of Conduct; and (3) tax and audit clients.

AUDIT FAILURES

Case 7.1
The Baptist Foundation of Arizona

Arthur Andersen LLP agreed to pay $217 million to settle a lawsuit over its audits for the Baptist Foundation of Arizona. This was the second largest settlement ever agreed to by a major accounting firm. The lawsuit alleged that Andersen accountants failed to detect fraudulent activity at the foundation. 11,000 people, most of them elderly investors, lost $570 million when the Baptist Foundation of Arizona filed for bankruptcy in 1999. The bankruptcy filing was one of the largest bankruptcy filings by a not-for-profit organization. With the money from Arthur Andersen and proceeds from the sale of foundation assets, investors are expected to recover about 70 cents for each dollar invested.

The Baptist Foundation of Arizona was founded in 1948 to raise money to support Baptist causes and to pay a return for investors. It filed for bankruptcy in 1999 after many of the foundation's executives had been convicted of criminal charges or indicted for fraud.

The lawsuit against Arthur Andersen alleged that Andersen auditors failed to detect fraudulent activity at the Baptist Foundation, including "hiding real-estate losses by transferring overvalued assets to shell companies in exchange for IOUs, and engaging in a Ponzi-like scheme of using new investor funds to make payments to previous investors."[1] A Ponzi scheme is an investment fraud where early investors are given returns from funds collected from later investors, even though no investment profits have yet been earned. When the trial began, *The Wall Street Journal* stated, "For Andersen, the question probably isn't whether the firm is liable at all, but rather how much it should be required to pay."[2]

Dan Guy, an expert witness called to testify against Andersen over the foundation audits, said, "Arthur Anderson did not live up to the minimum requirements in the rules set for auditors."[3] The lawsuit alleged that Arthur Andersen auditors did little to investigate allegations of fraud from whistle-blowers, and because of this omission they were complicit in keeping fraud concealed from investors. During the trial, Guy testified that he had reviewed Andersen working papers, as well as the depositions from the whistle-blowers, and determined that the fraud at the Baptist Foundation was not impenetrable. With the information from the whistle-blowers, Andersen had an obligation to gather evidence to investigate the charges. Citing a 1997 conversation between Baptist Foundation accountant Karen Paetz and Ann McGath, the Andersen auditor, McGath acknowledged that the client told her that the Baptist Foundation was selling overvalued assets to a related-party company. According to Guy's testimony, this kind of information would prompt a knowledgeable auditor to investigate further.

Additional evidence related to fraudulent activity that had been disclosed to the auditors was presented during the trial. Two chief financial officers of Texas Baptist Organization and a financial advisor from Mesa, Arizona, testified that they tried to alert Andersen to financial improprieties at the foundation and the likelihood that the foundation was broke.[4] Andersen had not responded to their calls.

Andersen placed the blame for the foundation collapse on the company's executives, the foundation's law firm, and the state regulators who failed to investigate investor complaints in the early 1990s. According to statements by Andersen executives, "There is clear evidence that all members of the Baptist Foundation's senior management and [a] majority of the Board of Directors engaged in a conspiracy of silence to deny information about the Baptist Foundation's financial condition to the Arthur Andersen auditors."[5]

The settlement came one week into the trial against Arthur Andersen, sparing Andersen from further court proceedings and allowing it to avoid potentially crippling punitive damages. Under the terms of the settlement, Andersen neither admits nor denies wrongdoing. In June 2002, Andersen paid the balance of the $217 million settlement, allowing Arthur Andersen to close the case brought against the firm in connection with the foundation audits.[6]

Questions

a. Identify the parties affected by the audit failure. Who benefited? Who is harmed?
b. Do you agree with the expert testimony stating the auditors should have uncovered the fraudulent activity?

124

c. What is the auditor's responsibility to investigate the allegations made by the whistle-blowers?

d. Discuss the auditor's responsibility for discovering fraud. Indicate what limits may be placed on this responsibility.

Case 7.2
Audit Methodology

A recent article in *The Wall Street Journal* reported on a study done by accounting researchers on auditing methodology. Researchers argued that auditors have changed their audit approaches over the last twenty years and these changes make it less likely that auditors will discover fraud by business executives. In the older style of auditing, the report argues, auditors looked at business transactions to determine whether the transactions were recorded properly, according to accounting rules. The new auditing methods, by contrast, focus on internal control. Relying on internal control documentation rather than reviewing transactions may catch fraud by low-level employees, the researchers claimed, but internal control can be circumvented by corporate executives. This means that high-level fraud is not easily discovered with contemporary audit procedures.[7]

Questions

a. As you understand these audit techniques, what is it within each procedure that may make it possible for auditors to detect fraud that is generated by either low-level or high-level employees?

b. What aspect of the audit industry may be driving the decisions to concentrate on internal control documentation? Don't auditors want to discover fraud that originates among high-level employees?

c. Do you think the real problems with fraud have to do with the "environment" within the particular company that pressures employees at each level to "go with the flow," and not to act ethically? Explain your reasoning.

(next page) - 7.3, 4, 5

7.7 - AIS

AICPA CODE OF PROFESSIONAL CONDUCT

Case 7.3
Ernst & Young Violations of Independence Rules

The Securities and Exchange Commission charged Ernst & Young with ethics code violations for engaging in lucrative business deals with an audit client.[8] Ernst & Young had entered into a marketing arrangement with PeopleSoft to sell and install PeopleSoft software. Under the agreement, Ernst & Young agreed to pay royalties to PeopleSoft of 15–30 percent for each software sale, with a minimum guaranteed payment of $300,000. During the time of this agreement, Ernst & Young served as the auditor for PeopleSoft. According to the SEC, "an auditor can't be in business to jointly generate revenues with an audit client without impairing independence." Ernst & Young vigorously contested the charges, saying that its work for PeopleSoft "was entirely appropriate and permissible under the profession's rules. It did not affect our client, its shareholders, or the investing public, nor is the SEC claiming any error in our audits or our client's financial statements as a result of them."

Questions

a. Evaluate the statement made by Ernst & Young that they did nothing wrong because no one was harmed. Is this an appropriate defense against a claim of lack of independence?
b. Develop an argument supporting the SEC's position. (The SEC independence code can be found at http://www.sec.gov/rules/final/33-7919.htm.)
c. Develop a counter argument supporting Ernst & Young's position.
d. If the position taken by Ernst & Young seems to violate the independence rules, why did Ernst & Young take this position?
e. Do you believe that the SEC or Ernst & Young will prevail?

Case 7.4
Ernst & Young Violations of Independence Rules

The Securities and Exchange Commission is investigating whether Ernst & Young may have violated accounting rules in their audit of Cendant.[9] According to SEC records, Ernst & Young proposed a "value bank" that gave Cendant a reduction in audit fees in return for consulting work. This proposal offered a reduction of the yearly audit fee in exchange for consideration of future consulting contracts for Cendant.

Questions

a. Does this arrangement appear to violate the code of professional conduct? Explain the violation.

b.   Why did Ernst & Young engage in this behavior if it violates the accounting rules? (Was the firm biased?)

Case 7.5
PricewaterhouseCoopers Independence Rule Violations

The SEC settled an independence case with PricewaterhouseCoopers (PWC) in July 2002.[10] The case found that from 1996 to 2001, PWC engaged in contingent fee arrangements with 14 public companies. In each instance, the client hired the audit firm's investment bankers to perform financial advisory services for a fee that was based on the success of the services. According to the SEC, this arrangement violated both the AICPA Code of Professional Conduct and the SEC independence rules. PWC agreed to pay the SEC $5 million and to provide independence training to all PWC professionals.

Questions

Identify the sections of the AICPA Code of Professional Conduct and the SEC Independence Code violated by the contingent fee arrangements. (The SEC independence code can be found at http://www.sec.gov/rules/final/33-7919.htm and the AICPA code is at http://www.aicpa.org/about/code/index.htm.
a.   Do you agree with the SEC finding?
b.   Why did PWC engage in this behavior if it violates the accounting rules?

Case 7.6
Independence Rules, AICPA Code of Professional Conduct

Using the AICPA Code of Professional Conduct, determine if independence is impaired in the following situations:
1. During the time of the audit, the spouse of the auditor has a direct interest in the client.
2. During the time of the audit, the auditor has a material indirect financial interest in the client.
3. During the time of the audit, the auditor had a loan from the client.
4. During the period of the professional engagement, the audit partner owned 8 percent of the client's stock.
5. Do the independence rules apply to an auditor's spouse, children, parents, brothers, and sisters?
6. If the audit partner's spouse works in the sales department for one of the auditor's clients, is the partner's independence impaired?
7. If the auditor authorizes client transactions, does this action impair independence?

8. If the auditor reports to the board of directors on behalf of management, is independence impaired?

9. If the auditor serves as the stock transfer agent for his client, is independence impaired?

Case 7.7
Independence and the Installation of Accounting Information Systems

If the CPA is hired to design or install information systems for a client, describe activities that will not impair independence and activities that will impair independence.

Case 7.8
Loans from Audit Clients

Is a CPA permitted to have a car loan from its audit client? How about a credit card debt from an audit client?

Case 7.9
Mortgages from Audit Clients

Is a CPA permitted to accept an audit engagement for the mortgage company holding his or her home mortgage?

Case 7.10
Client Litigation and Audit Contracts

If you are involved in litigation with your audit client, can you be hired to audit the financial statements for the following year?

Case 7.11
Internal Audit Services Performed by CPA

Can a CPA perform the internal audit function for his or her audit client? If so, what internal control decisions remain the responsibility of the client?

Case 7.12
Definitions of Family and Relatives

Define *close relative, covered member,* and *immediate family* as used by the AICPA Code of Professional Conduct. Give one example of how these terms are used in the code.

Case 7.13
CPA Participation in Investment Clubs

Can a CPA join an investment club? Are there any restrictions in stock ownership for the investment club?

Case 7.14
Client Gifts

If you accept a gift from a client, have you violated the code of professional conduct?

Case 7.15
Lack of Industry Knowledge

You have been hired to audit a company in an industry where you have no industry knowledge. Does the fact that you will have to research the industry or consult with other professionals to gain knowledge regarding the industry mean that you have violated the professional competence requirement of the code of conduct?

Case 7.16
Contingent Fee Arrangements

List two situations when a contingent fee arrangement would be permitted by the code of professional conduct.

Case 7.17
The Use of Outside Service Bureaus to Process Tax Returns

Can you use an outside service bureau to process tax returns for clients? Is this a violation of client confidentiality?

Case 7.18
Disclosure of Client Names

Can a CPA disclose the name of a client for whom the member performed professional services, or is this considered to be confidential client information?

Case 7.19
Failure of CPA to File State Tax Return

You fail to file a state tax return in 2003. Have you violated the code of professional conduct by your action? Have you committed an act discreditable to the profession when you fail to pay the payroll taxes for your gardener?

Case 7.20
Discrimination Lawsuit Filed Against CPA Firm

One of your employees has filed a discrimination lawsuit against the firm. If you are found to be guilty in a court of law, have you also violated the code of professional conduct by engaging in discriminatory practices?

Case 7.21
Giving a Clean Opinion on Statements that Are Not Materially Correct

You know that the financial statements for the client you are auditing are not materially correct, but you sign off on the audit opinion without requiring the client to make the corrections. Have you violated the code of professional conduct by your actions?

Case 7.22
Disclosure of Information Related to the CPA Exam

One of your friends has just finished taking the CPA exam. You are particularly interested in the type of questions that appear in the auditing section and ask the friend to describe the essay questions. Have you violated the professional code of conduct by your action?

Case 7.23
Withholding Client Statements for Non Payment of Fees

Your client has requested that you return the monthly bank statements for the year that you obtained from the client and used in the audit. You have not been paid by the client for the work you did on the audit and you do not want to return the statements.

Questions

a. Are you in violation of the code of professional conduct by retaining the client's records?
b. Are there any situations that allow you to keep the client records?

Case 7.24
Providing the Client with Copies of the Audit Workpapers

Your client has requested that you provide them with a copy of your workpapers for their file. They believe that if they have this copy, they will be better prepared next year for the audit.

Questions

a. Does the code of professional conduct require you to provide your client with a copy of your workpapers?

Case 7.25
Providing the Client with Copies of the Tax Timing Difference Worksheet

Your client has requested a copy of the schedule describing the tax timing differences that is a part of your workpapers. You maintain this copy in paper form and they would like a computer version of the spreadsheet.

Questions

a. If you do not provide your client with this information, have you violated the code professional conduct?
b. If you provide the information and the client loses the spreadsheet and requests a second copy of the material after two months, are you in violation of the code of professional conduct if you do not provide the requested information?

Case 7.26
Lowballing a Client Bid

You are preparing a bid for a new client and plan to lowball the bid to get the client. You know that the fee is almost always adjusted at the end of the audit due to nonperformance on the part of the client, so you are not concerned that you would be unable to make a profit on the initial bid.

Questions

a. Does this practice of bidding low on the engagement fees to get the client violate the code of professional conduct?

Case 7.27
CPA Influence on IRS

A CPA is contacted by a client to represent them on a hearing for a tax dispute with the IRS. In discussion with the client, the CPA stresses her extensive experience with the IRS. Because of this experience, she explains to the potential client that she will be able to influence the IRS to reduce the tax liability for the client.

Questions

a. Has the CPA violated the code of professional conduct?
b. Describe the statements a CPA could make to the client in this situation.

Case 7.28
Providing Referrals to Audit Clients

A former audit client calls and asks for a recommendation for someone to install a new accounting software package. You provide a referral for the service. Under what conditions can you charge a fee for the referral?

Case 7.29
AICPA Code of Professional Conduct and Corporate Accountants

The ethics code of the American Institute of Certified Public Accountants requires industry CPAs to inform on their employers if they believe that the company's financial statements are "materially misstated." Under the code, if industry CPAs believe their company's financial statement are materially misstated, they are expected to report their concerns regarding the accuracy of the financial statements to their supervisors. If their supervisors fail to take corrective action, accountants must consider reporting the misstatements to the auditors of the company and the Securities and Exchange Commission. Industry CPAs could lose their licenses if they fail to comply with these requirements. They might also be sued by company stockholders for failing to protect stockholder interests.

Questions

a.   This change seems to require that the industry CPA's first obligation is not to his or her employer, but rather to the code professional conduct. What difficulties are associated with this change?
b.   What is the ethical dilemma faced by accountants who must choose between their employers (their jobs) and their profession (who they are)?
c.   Identify the interested parties involved in this decision. Who benefits by the change? Who is harmed?
d.   As an industry accountant, what would you do if faced with this dilemma? Why?

Case 7.30
Disclosing Client Information

Anne Sorenson, an auditor for KPMG, is working on the audit of Amgen, Inc. Amgen is a biotechnology company based in Thousand Oaks, California. The audit has been fairly calm so far, but today Anne overheard a very exciting piece of information. Amgen has just completed a series of tests with mice related to the *ob* gene and leptin, the protein produced by the gene. During these tests, obese mice lost about 40 percent of their body weight after only a month of daily injections of leptin. With trials on humans ready to begin within a year, the promise of a cure for obesity seems hopeful. That evening, Anne is talking to her parents over the phone. She is so excited about this finding that she tells her parents about the potential cure for obesity. After getting off the phone, Anne is telling her roommate about her interesting day, when she realizes that she is divulging confidential client information. Her roommate, a stockbroker at Merrill Lynch, is excited about the information and wants to recommend that all her investment customers purchase Amgen stock before the information is public and the stock price goes up. Anne wonders about what she has just done.

Questions

a. What is the ethical dilemma described in this problem?

b. Identify the interested parties affected by this decision. Who benefits? Who is harmed?

c. Based on your knowledge of auditing standards and the AICPA Code of Professional Conduct, has Anne acted ethically?

d. Would your evaluation of Anne's behavior change if her roommate was an artist who was uninterested in the stock market or if her parents did not act on the information to purchase Amgen stock? Why?

Case 7.31
Tax Return Preparation by Big Four Accounting Firms

According to a recent article in *The Wall Street Journal,* the Big Four audit firms earn approximately 20 percent of their total revenue from tax preparation. The article reported that Big Four accounting firms used temporary workers and part-time employees to prepare tax returns in the current tax season, sometimes setting up separate "compliance centers" staffed by temporary employees and shipping returns to these central locations for processing. The temporary workers are paid as little as $10 per hour, but the clients are billed at the rate for Big Four employees, as much as $100 per hour or more. Most firms hide their use of temporary employees, because they believe their clients are "indifferent" about who prepares their return as long as it is signed by a partner or manager of a Big Four firm. The head of the tax division for one of the firms says that they see no reason to advise a client that a temporary employee filled out their tax return. "It doesn't seem relevant." This leads clients to believe they are receiving the services of accountants with "elite credentials" whenever they pay the premium fee charged by the Big Four accounting firms. A tax client of one of the firms, when informed of this practice, said that he is generally satisfied with the work the firm has done. He had known that the tax partner signing the return didn't actually prepare it. "But in all honesty, they should tell the clients" about mailing their tax data to temporary employees in other cities. Another client, when learning of this practice, said: "That's not a very ethical thing to do. They should have told me."

Questions

a. Is it unethical for Big Four accounting firms to hire part-time and temporary workers to prepare tax returns? What is the ethical dilemma described in this case?
b. Do you believe that all clients are indifferent about who prepares their returns as long as a Big Four manager or partner signs the return?
c. Why are Big Four firms engaging in this practice? Do they really believe that the client doesn't care?
d. What parties should be considered in making this decision? Who benefits? Who is harmed?
e. What would you do? Can you suggest some alternatives to make this situation more ethical?

Case 7.32
Clients Dropped by Big Four Firms

A recent article in *The Wall Street Journal* reported that the Big Four accounting firms are dropping risky clients from their client base in an effort to reduce legal costs. New companies, which have the highest failure rate and are the riskiest to audit, are the most likely to be dropped. However, older companies are also subject to being cut loose by their auditor if they are deemed to be a high risk in terms of potential lawsuits. Accounting firms say they have no choice, with lawsuit settlement costs now exceeding $1 billion per year, a figure that represents 12 percent of their audit revenue. Clients say they are being denied the "Good Housekeeping Seal of Approval" when Big Four auditors refuse to audit their firms. Some Big Four firms are also requesting that clients sign indemnification clauses requiring the client to pay the court costs if the auditor is sued by a third party, or agreeing to resolve disputes by arbitration or mediation rather than a lawsuit.[11]

Questions

a. What is the ethical dilemma discussed in this case?
b. Is it true that accounting firms have no choice but to drop the "risky clients"?
c. Identify the interested parties involved in this decision. Who benefits? Who is harmed?
d. What would you do if you were asked to send a termination letter to one of your audit clients?

Endnotes

[1] Anne Brady, "Andersen: Called to account: Andersen pays foundation investors," *The Wall Street Journal*, June 6, 2002.

[2] Jonathan Weil, "Andersen Trial with Baptist Foundation set to begin," *The Wall Street Journal*, April 29, 2002.

[3] Anne Brady, "Andersen was lax in auditing of Baptist group, witness says," *The Wall Street Journal*, May 2, 2002.

[4] Ibid.

[5] Jonathan Weil, "U.S. will Argue," *The Wall Street Journal*, May 7, 2002.

[6] Anne Brady, "Andersen: Called to account: Andersen pays foundation investors," *The Wall Street Journal*, June 6, 2002.

[7] Ken Brown, "Auditors' methods make it hard to catch fraud by executives," *The Wall Street Journal*, July 8, 2002.

[8] Michael Schroeder and Scot J. Paltrow, "SEC says Ernst & Young violated Independence Rules in Past Audits," *The Wall Street Journal*, May 21, 2002.

[9] Michael Schroeder and Scot J. Paltrow, "SEC says Ernst & Young violated Independence Rules in Past Audits," *The Wall Street Journal*, May 21, 2002.

[10] "PricewaterhouseCoopers Settles SEC Auditor Independence Case," U.S. Securities and Exchange Commission, http:// www.sec.gov/news/press/2002-105.htm.

[11] Lee Berton, "Big accounting firms weed out risky clients," *The Wall Street Journal*, June 26, 1995.